Buffet at Fort Aguada Beach Resort, Goa.
Page I\ From front: Green Curry of Fish, recipe page 58; Red Curry of Beef, recipe page 35; Chicken Curry with Shrimp Paste, recipe page 75.

THE COMPLETE CURRY COOKBOOK

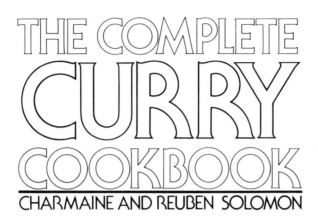

THE COMPLETE CURRY COOKBOOK

CHARMAINE AND REUBEN SOLOMON

Photography by Reg Morrison and Ray Joyce

McGRAW-HILL BOOK COMPANY
New York St. Louis San Francisco Toronto

ACKNOWLEDGEMENTS

I would like to thank the following for their part in providing artifacts, utensils and ingredients used in photography: Mrs Ava Newman of The Kansu Gallery, 605 Royal Arcade, Hilton Hotel, Sydney for the magnificent Buddha in the photograph on page 1, The Tourist Organisation of Thailand, The Thai Trade Centre, The Indian Tourist Office, Mrs Ida Htoon Phay, The N.S.W. Fish Marketing Authority.

But most of all I want to thank my husband, Reuben, whose help I enlisted in the preparation of this book and who has worked very hard to make it good. He really is the greatest curry enthusiast I know and has a flair for creating dishes with a clever use of spices. Why waste such talent? He has learned to walk a fine line between his carefree improvisations as a cook and the careful measuring and committing to paper, to which every cookery writer must submit. And so, when you enjoy the results of your cooking from these recipes, I cannot take all the credit — Reuben take a bow!

Edited by Peita Royle
Designed and illustrated by Ann Twells
First published in 1980 by
Lansdowne Press Sydney
176 South Creek Road, Dee Why West, NSW, Australia 2099
© Copyright Charmaine Solomon 1980
Produced in Australia by the Publisher
Typeset in New Zealand by Jacobsen Typesetters Ltd.
Printed in Hong Kong by South China Printing Co.

LIBRARY OF CONGRESS CATALOGING IN PUBLICATION DATA

Solomon, Charmaine.
  The complete curry cook book.

  Includes Index.
  1. Cookery (Curry) I. Solomon, Reuben, joint author.
II. Royle, Peita. III. Title
TX819.C9S64 1981   641.6′384   80-27459
ISBN 0-07-059639-5

contents

Basics of curry cooking

In most curries, besides spices, there are ingredients you will be using repeatedly so let's become familiar with them.

Onions   Almost every curry includes onions. In Asia, the onions are mainly purplish red, rather like the true shallot, the small bulb that grows in clusters like garlic. Since these are not always available we have used brown or white onions. These vary so much in size that for guidance in helping you decide what we mean by a large or medium onion, a large onion is 250 g (8 oz) or more; a medium onion is about 125 g (4 oz) and a small onion is around 60 g (2 oz). The next time you buy onions, weigh some of different sizes to obtain an idea of the variation. But don't bother to weigh your onions each time you cook a curry. It's not all that crucial.

Garlic   Garlic cloves can vary from tiny ones the size of a pistachio nut to big ones about the size of a walnut! To introduce uniformity we adopted the method of chopping garlic and measuring it in spoonfuls. Since the garlic is usually chopped anyway before cooking, this does not entail extra work.

Ginger   The Asian way of calling for a slice or two of ginger, or a 'thumb-sized' piece of ginger gives too much leeway so again we have called for chopped or grated ginger root, measured in standard spoons.

Chillies, Fresh   Fresh chillies are used in most Asian food. For mild curries, the whole chilli is added while simmering, then lifted out and discarded. But for an authentic fiery quality the chillies should be chopped or perhaps ground in the electric blender. If you leave the seeds in the flavour will be hotter than if you remove the seeds. Either way, equip yourself with disposable plastic gloves or well-fitting rubber gloves because chillies can be so hot that even repeated washings will not stop the tingling sensation that will result if your skin comes into contact with the juices.

Having protected your hands, remove stalk of chilli and make a slit to remove the seeds, scraping them out with the tip of a knife. Or cut the chilli in two lengthways and remove the central membrane together with the seeds. Remember, do not touch your face, your eyes or young children after handling chillies — it is an experience you won't forget!

Chillies, Dried   There are large and small dried chillies. The smaller they are, the hotter they are. Those called for in these recipes are the large variety, and they still have plenty of heat and flavour.

Break off the stem end of the dried chilli and if you don't want too much heat, shake so that the seeds fall out. Soak for 10 minutes or so in hot water before grinding. Dried chillies, though they give plenty of oomph, do not have as much effect on the skin as fresh chillies with their volatile oils.

Until they have been soaked and ground they are safe enough to handle. But following this process, remember to wash your hands at once with soap and water.

Coconut Milk   There are so many ways to get coconut milk other than from a fresh coconut . . . canned, concentrated or 'creamed' coconut, frozen and so on.

For convenience you may use canned coconut milk for the recipes in this book. Make sure, however, that you purchase a good brand. It should be white in colour, not grey. And the smell should be fresh and sweet. Not all canned coconut milks are created equal. Be choosey. The concentrated creamed coconut is also convenient and should be dissolved in water, about 60 g (2 oz) creamed coconut and enough water to make up 1 cup (8 fl oz) makes a medium strength coconut milk. Use more for 'thick' milk and less for 'thin' milk.

One of the best and most reliable methods is extracting coconut milk from desiccated coconut (dried, shredded coconut).

Coconut milk is extracted in two stages. The first yield being the 'thick' milk, the second 'thin milk'. Use a mixture of first and second extracts when a recipe calls for coconut milk, unless thick milk or thin milk is specified. Sometimes they are added at different stages of the recipe. In some recipes you use 'coconut cream'. This is the rich layer that rises to the top of the thick milk (or first extract) after it has been left to stand for a while. If the coconut cream is to be cooked down to make an oily substance, as for instance in the Thai curry pastes, this is one time you should not use canned coconut milk, as it contains a stabilizer and instead of turning to oil you end up with crunchy brown bits of dried coconut milk which are very nice to nibble, but totally unsuitable for the purpose of the recipe.

Using Desiccated Coconut: Put 2 cups (6 oz) desiccated coconut in a large bowl and pour 2½ cups (20 fl oz) hot water over. Allow to cool to lukewarm, then knead firmly with the hand for a few minutes and strain through a fine strainer or a piece of muslin, squeezing out as much liquid as possible. This should yield about 1½ cups (12 fl oz) thick coconut milk.

Using the same coconut and 2½ cups (20 fl oz) more hot water, repeat the process. Knead well and squeeze really hard to get all the moisture and flavour from the coconut. This will yield approximately 2 cups (16 fl oz) thin coconut milk. (Because of the moisture retained in the coconut after the first extract, the second extract usually yields more milk.)

Using a blender: With an electric blender you save time and a lot of hard kneading and squeezing. Put 2 cups (6 fl oz) desiccated coconut and 2½ cups (20 fl oz) hot water in blender container, cover and blend for 30 seconds on high speed. Strain through a fine sieve or piece of muslin, squeezing out all the moisture. Repeat process, using the same coconut and 2½ cups (20 fl oz) more hot water.

Using fresh coconut: In Asian countries, fresh coconut is used. It may be bought ready grated from the markets, but a coconut grater is stan-dard equipment in every household. If you can buy a coconut grater at one of the Asian stores, well and good. If you can't, the blender comes to the rescue again.

But let's start with the coconut. First crack the nut in two by hitting it with the back of a heavy kitchen chopper on the middle of the nut. Tap hard several times, going round the 'equator' of the coconut. Once a crack has appeared, insert the thin edge of a blade and prise it open. Save the sweet liquid inside for drinking. (This is *not* coconut milk, though it is commonly referred to as such in western books.) Put the two halves of the nut into a low oven and in 15 or 20 minutes the flesh will start to come away from the shell. Lift out with the point of a knife, peel away the thin dark brown skin that clings to the white meat. Cut into chunks, put into a container of electric blender with 2 cups (16 fl oz) water and blend at a high speed until coconut is completely pulverised. Strain out liquid, repeat using more water and same coconut.

To extract fresh coconut milk by hand, grate the pieces of white meat finely and to each cup of grated coconut add a cup (8 fl oz) of hot water, knead thoroughly and strain out the liquid. Repeat process a second and even a third time, adding hot water.

presentation of curry

Just as Far Eastern food tastes better when eaten with chopsticks, so the food of India and South East Asia tastes better eaten with the fingers. Rice or unleavened bread is most often served with spicy curries and other accompaniments. And the only way to manage the flat breads is by tearing off pieces and using them to scoop up the curries. Rice is usually served with spoon and fork, though the purists prefer to use the fingers of the right hand. There is a knack to it which may need a little practice for the novice.

More important than 'how to' is 'how much'. In other words, a good meal is mainly a matter of proportions, and this is where the inexperienced Westerner comes undone. In Western meals it is the meat, fish or poultry which is the main item. In Asian meals, rice or bread such as chapatis or rotis form the main part of the meal, while the spicy curries and accompaniments are meant to be eaten in smaller quantities. Certainly there should be three or four times as much rice as curry, for the spiciness of curry is cushioned by the neutral rice and no discomfort is felt afterwards. If rice is relegated to a minor role the richness of the curries may prove too much for the average digestion.

All the food is brought to the table at once. Rice should be served with a meat or poultry curry, with a fish or other seafood curry and with two or more vegetable curries. On festive occasions beef, pork, chicken, prawns are served at the same meal, each one prepared in a different style. Accompaniments are served in smaller quantities, and indeed, the more pungent and strongly flavoured they are, the smaller the amount that should be placed on the table and the smaller the spoon should be to serve them. Some very hot sambals we serve with a coffee spoon as an indication these are only the accents to the meal and should be approached with caution. But if your guests are not accustomed to Asian food, don't rely on the subtle hint of small portions and spoons; come right out and warn them that such and such a dish is hot with chillies or they may find themselves in much discomfort.

Pappadams, the popular lentil wafers which are served with Indian or Sri Lankan meals, should always be placed on a separate small plate like a bread and butter plate. Otherwise the steam from the hot food will cause their delightful crispness to diminish.

Etiquette (and commonsense) decree that rice is served first in the centre of the plate. Curries and accompaniments are placed around it in much smaller quantities. The impression that rice and all the curries should be mixed together is quite wrong. Each different accompaniment or curry should be tasted separately, with a mouthful of rice or piece of chapati.

What to drink with a curry meal? Cool water is ideal. But if you prefer an alcoholic beverage, please consider ice-cold lager or other light ale. A beer shandy is particularly nice.

For wine drinkers, a light wine punch such as sangria is delicious or a very fruity white wine. Avoid dry wines, particularly red wines. Fine wines are lost when served with highly spiced food and a dry wine does nothing to complement a good curry.

Or serve mango juice or rose-flavoured syrup poured over crushed ice. It is ideal for sipping with a curry meal.

CURRy pastes and spice combinations

We do not recommend using a standard curry powder because it will produce a sameness in all your curries. But certain combinations of fragrant spices, herbs and whole, unground seeds add such a marvellous aromatic accent, they are very useful to have on hand.

For instance, the combination of five seeds (*panch phora*) used in Indian cooking is all that is necessary to transport a vegetable from blandness to sheer delight. The seeds, combined in certain proportions and used whole, not ground, are tossed in a small quantity of hot oil or ghee to release the flavours which then permeate the vegetable during cooking.

Then there are ground spice mixes (*garam masalas*) which emphasize and enhance flavours. They are impractical to make in the very small amounts called for in each recipe, so I advise grinding a quantity and storing it airtight and away from heat and light. It will retain its flavour and fragrance for months if stored in the freezer.

The fresh herbs used in green masala paste are not always in season, and one should therefore prepare a few bottles when they are available. This preserves them in oil for use later on. Green masala paste may be used to add a flavour change to basic Indian curries, or it may be used on its own.

As you use this book you'll find that while some of the spices are common to the cooking of most Asian countries, there are others that are very definitely confined to one area. This applies particularly to fresh herbs such as fenugreek (popular in India but not in South East Asia). On the other hand, lemon grass (*serai*) and pandan (*rampé*) which are almost universally used in South East Asian cuisine and even in Sri Lanka which is so close, geographically, to India, are never used in Indian food.

Even different parts of the same plant are favoured according to the country we visit. The fresh green leaves of coriander herb are found in the cooking of India, and all the way east to China, except in Sri Lanka where it is looked upon with disfavour because of its pungent smell. But in Thailand, where the root of the plant is used in combination with garlic and black pepper, this is considered of greater importance than the leaves.

Although we would never advocate using the same spice mixture for any and every curry, for convenience a small amount of a good curry powder comes in handy. You can, of course, buy one. Many good mixtures are sold commercially, but there are also many that lack flavour because of a skimping on the more expensive spices and a reliance on 'fillers' such as rice flour, to make up the bulk. 'Curry powder' is scorned in Asian countries, housewives and cooks preferring to make their own combinations.

When buying a commercial curry powder, check that it comes in tins or bottles and is not packed in cardboard or plastic. Much of the flavour and aromatic oils are quickly dissipated when packed in those materials.

If you are pressed for time and wish to have a curry meal, use a good curry paste or a canned commercial curry powder, but do not stop at that. By adding small quantities of your favourite spices you will enhance and vary the flavour of that particular curry powder.

Making your own curry powder is vastly more satisfying if you are a true curry enthusiast — and you must be, or you would not be reading this. We are including recipes for some curry blends, but even if you like them very much do remember these are not to be relied on every time you cook a curry.

Curries and other spiced dishes must have distinctive character. This is the reason we have mostly used individual spices in the recipes that follow. When cooking a curry, the cook with his spices is like an artist with his palette full of colours, mixed together to create his masterpiece.

In this book we have given you our own special recipes for the curries. Use them as a starting point, because we've tested them and found that's how we like them. But by all means feel free to be the artist the second time around, and improvise. We wish you happy cooking and good eating.

INDIA
PANCH PHORA

'Panch' means five in Hindi, and panch phora is a combination of five different aromatic seeds. These are used whole and, when added to the cooking oil, impart a flavour typical of certain Indian dishes.

2 tablespoons black mustard seed
2 tablespoons cummin seed
2 tablespoons black cummin seed
1 tablespoon fenugreek seed
1 tablespoon fennel seed

Put all ingredients into a glass jar with a tight-fitting lid. Shake before using to ensure an even distribution.

INDIA
GARAM MASALA

Sprinkle a teaspoon of this over a curry before serving — the result is breathtaking. **Reuben.**

4 tablespoons coriander seeds
2 tablespoons cummin seeds
1 tablespoon whole black peppercorns
**2 teaspoons cardamom seeds (measure after
  removing pods)**
4 x 7.5 cm (3 in) cinnamon sticks
1 teaspoon whole cloves
1 whole nutmeg

In a small pan roast separately the coriander, cummin, peppercorns, cardamom, cinnamon and cloves. As each one starts to smell fragrant turn on to a plate to cool. Put all into electric blender and blend to a fine powder. Finely grate nutmeg and mix in. Store in a glass jar with an airtight lid.

SRI LANKA
FRAGRANT SPICE POWDER

2 teaspoons whole cloves
1 tablespoon cardamom seeds
1 tablespoon whole black peppercorns
2 tablespoons broken cinnamon stick
4 tablespoons cummin seeds

Roast these spices for 5 minutes in a dry pan over medium heat. Cool slightly and grind to a very fine consistency in an electric blender on high speed. Sprinkle a teaspoon of this powder over game or meat curries just before serving. Bottle and store away from heat and sunlight.

THAILAND
GREEN CURRY PASTE

4 large fresh green chillies
1 teaspoon black peppercorns
1 small brown onion, chopped
1 tablespoon chopped garlic
2 tablespoons chopped fresh coriander plant,
   including root
1 stem fresh lemon grass, sliced or
   2 teaspoons chopped lemon rind
1 teaspoon salt
2 teaspoons ground coriander
1 teaspoon ground cummin
1 teaspoon serai powder
1 teaspoon laos powder
2 teaspoons dried shrimp paste
1 teaspoon ground turmeric
1 tablespoon oil

Remove stems of chillies, and leave the seeds in if you want the curry paste to be hot. Roughly chop the chillies and put into container of electric blender together with all other ingredients. Blend to a smooth paste, turning off motor and scraping down sides of blender with a spatula and adding a little extra oil or a tablespoon of water if necessary.

INDIA
MADRAS CURRY PASTE

1 cup (2⅔ oz) ground coriander
½ cup (1⅓ oz) ground cummin
1 tablespoon each ground black pepper, turmeric,
   black mustard, chilli powder, and salt
2 tablespoons each crushed garlic and finely grated
   fresh ginger
vinegar for mixing
¾ cup (6 fl oz) oil

Combine ground spices and salt in a bowl. Add garlic and ginger and sufficient vinegar to mix to a smooth, thick purée. Heat oil in saucepan and when very hot turn in the spice mixture and reduce heat. Stir constantly until spices are cooked and oil separates from spices. Cool and bottle.

Use about a tablespoon of this paste for each 500 g (1 lb) of meat, fish or poultry, substituting it for the garlic, ginger and spices in a recipe.

SRI LANKA
CEYLON CURRY PASTE

1 cup (3 oz) coriander seeds
¼ cup (¾ oz) cummin seeds
2 teaspoons fennel seeds
2 teaspoons fenugreek seeds
2 tablespoons ground rice
2 tablespoons desiccated coconut
12 dried red chillies
2 cinnamon sticks, broken
2 teaspoons cardamom seeds
2 teaspoons whole cloves
2 tablespoons chopped garlic
1 tablespoon chopped fresh ginger
vinegar and water for blending
16 dried curry leaves
3 rampé, cut into 5 cm (2 in) lengths

Over medium low heat, dry roast separately the coriander, cummin, fennel and fenugreek, stirring constantly until each one smells fragrant and turns fairly dark brown. Set aside to cool. Roast ground rice and coconut to a light brown colour and set aside to cool.

Place all roasted ingredients into electric blender container, add chillies, cinnamon, cardamom, cloves, garlic and ginger. Blend to a smooth paste, adding a little liquid to assist movement of blades. Remove paste from container and combine with curry leaves and rampé. Store in a screw-top glass jar in refrigerator.

Use 2 tablespoons paste to every 500 g (1 lb) of meat or poultry. Proceed as for **Curry Paste for Poultry** (see page 17).

INDIA

MADRAS CURRY POWDER

1 cup (3 oz) coriander seeds
½ cup (1½ oz) cummin seeds
¼ cup (¾ oz) fennel seeds
¼ cup (⅔ oz) black mustard seeds
¼ cup (⅓ oz) dried red chillies (broken)
2 tablespoons whole black peppercorns
2 teaspoons fenugreek seeds
1 tablespoon ground turmeric
20 dried curry leaves

In a dry pan roast separately all ingredients, except the turmeric and curry leaves, until they smell fragrant. Grind all ingredients to a fine powder in an electric blender. Mix in ground turmeric, bottle and store in freezer or other cool, dry place.

Note: Use 1-2 tablespoons of powder to each 500 g (1 lb) of main ingredient.

INDIA

GREEN MASALA PASTE

A spice paste based on fresh coriander leaves, mint, garlic and ginger. Added to any curry or special preparation, it will give extra flavour. It does not take the place of curry paste or individual spices.

1 teaspoon fenugreek seeds
5 large cloves garlic
2 tablespoons finely chopped fresh ginger
1 cup (1½ oz) firmly packed fresh mint leaves
1 cup (1½ oz) firmly packed fresh coriander leaves
½ cup (4 fl oz) vinegar
3 teaspoons salt
2 teaspoons ground turmeric
½ teaspoon ground cloves
1 teaspoon ground cardamom
½ cup (4 fl oz) vegetable oil
¼ cup (2 fl oz) sesame oil

Put fenugreek seeds in water to soak overnight. They will swell and develop a jelly-like coating. Measure 1 teaspoon of soaked seeds and put into container of electric blender with garlic, ginger, mint, coriander and vinegar. Blend on high speed until very smooth. Mix in salt and ground spices.

Heat oils until very hot, add blended mixture, bring to boil, turn off heat. Cool and bottle. Oil should cover the top of the herbs. If there is not quite enough oil, heat a little more and add it to the bottle.

MALAYSIA

CURRY PASTE FOR BEEF OR PORK

¾ cup (2¼ oz) coriander seeds
2 tablespoons cummin seeds
¼ cup (⅓ oz) dried red chillies, broken
2 teaspoons ground turmeric
5 candle nuts *or* 4 brazil kernels, chopped
1 teaspoon laos powder
6 teaspoons chopped garlic
3 teaspoons chopped fresh ginger
4 stems fresh lemon grass, chopped *or* rind of one lemon
1 tablespoon black peppercorns
3 teaspoons salt
vinegar and water for blending

Place all ingredients in container of electric blender. Add a little liquid to facilitate movement of the blades and blend to a smooth paste. Allow to cool and store in a screw-top glass jar in refrigerator.

Allow 2 tablespoons of paste to every 500 g (1 lb) meat. Proceed as for **Curry Paste for Poultry** (see page 17).

SRI LANKA

CEYLON CURRY POWDER

1 cup (3 oz) coriander seeds
½ cup (1½ oz) cummin seeds
1 tablespoon fennel seeds
1 teaspoon fenugreek seeds
1 cinnamon stick, about 5 cm (2 in)
1 teaspoon whole cloves
1 teaspoon cardamom seeds
2 tablespoons dried curry leaves
2 teaspoons chilli powder, optional
2 tablespoons ground rice, optional

In a dry pan over low heat roast *separately* the coriander, cummin, fennel and fenugreek, stirring constantly until each one becomes a fairly dark brown. Do not let them burn.

Put this mixture into blender container together with cinnamon stick broken in pieces, the cloves, cardamom and curry leaves. Blend on high speed until finely powdered. Combine with chilli powder and ground rice if used. Store in an airtight jar.

MALAYSIA

CURRY PASTE FOR FISH & SHELLFISH

½ cup (1½ oz) coriander seeds
1 tablespoon cummin seeds
2 teaspoons fennel seeds
¼ cup (⅓ oz) dried chillies, broken
6 teaspoons chopped garlic
4 teaspoons chopped fresh ginger
5 candle nuts *or* 4 brazil kernels, chopped
1 teaspoon kencur
2 tablespoons desiccated coconut
3 teaspoons blachan
2 teaspoons tamarind paste
1 teaspoon laos powder
3 teaspoons salt
2 teaspoons ground turmeric
4 stems fresh lemon grass, chopped *or*
   rind of 1 lemon
water for blending

Place all ingredients in container of electric blender. Add a little water to facilitate movement of the blades, and blend to a smooth paste. Allow to cool and store in a screw-top glass jar in refrigerator.

Allow 2 tablespoons of paste to every 500 g (1 lb) sea-food. Proceed as for **Curry Paste for Poultry** (see recipe below)

MALAYSIA

CURRY PASTE FOR POULTRY

½ cup (1½ oz) coriander seeds
1 tablespoon cummin seeds
2 teaspoons sweet cummin seeds
¼ cup (⅓ oz) dried red chillies, broken
5 candle nuts *or* 4 brazil kernels, chopped
3 stems fresh lemon grass, finely sliced *or*
   rind of 1 lemon
4 teaspoons chopped garlic
4 teaspoons chopped fresh ginger
2 teaspoons laos powder
3 teaspoons salt
water for blending

Place all ingredients in container of electric blender. Add a little water to facilitate movement of the blades, and blend to a smooth paste. Allow to cool and store in a screw-top glass jar in refrigerator.

Allow 1-2 tablespoons paste to every 500 g (1 lb) poultry. Slice one onion and fry till soft and brown, then add paste. Fry till mixture smells fragrant and oil comes to the surface. Stir in ½ cup (4 fl oz) hot water to mixture, cover and simmer for 10 minutes. Add poultry pieces, stir well with mixture and simmer covered till meat is tender. Serve with boiled rice.

THAILAND
RED CURRY PASTE

RED CURRY PASTE Thailand

4-6 dried red chillies
2 small brown onions, chopped
1 teaspoon black peppercorns
2 teaspoons ground cummin
1 tablespoon ground coriander
2 tablespoons chopped fresh coriander plant,
  including root
1 teaspoon salt
2 teaspoons chopped lemon rind
1 teaspoon serai powder
1 teaspoon laos powder
1 tablespoon chopped garlic
2 teaspoons dried shrimp paste
1 tablespoon oil
1 teaspoon turmeric
2 teaspoons paprika

Remove stems from chillies, but keep the seeds in if you want the curry paste to be as hot as it is in Thailand. Break the chillies into pieces and put into container of an electric blender together with all the other ingredients. Blend to a smooth paste, stopping motor frequently and pushing ingredients on to blades. It may be necessary to add a tablespoon of water or extra oil.

THAILAND
MOSLEM CURRY PASTE

You can make this curry paste two ways — either using the whole spices, roasting and grinding them (you will need a stout mortar and pestle for this) or by using the ground spices. Since, in some areas it is easier to buy whole spices than in others where one can only obtain ground spices, I have tested this recipe using both forms. One is just as successful as the other, and the ground spices certainly require less effort.

7-10 dried chillies *or* 2 teaspoons chilli powder
2 tablespoons coriander seeds *or* ground coriander
1 teaspoon cummin *or* fennel seeds *or* ground fennel
2 teaspoons laos powder, optional
1 teaspoon shredded lemon grass *or* finely peeled
  lemon rind
5 whole cloves *or* ¼ teaspoon ground cloves
1 stick cinnamon *or* 1 teaspoon ground cinnamon
5 cardamom pods *or* ½ teaspoon ground cardamom
1 blade mace *or* ½ teaspoon ground mace
2 tablespoons oil
2 medium-sized onions, finely sliced
2½ teaspoons finely chopped garlic
½ teaspoon dried shrimp paste

Break the chillies, shake out the seeds, and roast them lightly in a dry pan. Pound in a mortar and pestle. Roast the coriander seeds until aromatic and dark brown, shaking pan frequently or stirring. Pound in a mortar until seeds are reduced to fine powder (if spices are pounded while hot, they are easily pulverised). Roast cummin seeds until they crackle and start to pop, then grind to a powder. I have not suggested grinding them in a blender because the quantities are so small there is not enough for the blades to work on.

If using ground spices, dry-roast the ground coriander and fennel over low heat, stirring constantly and taking care they do not burn. Roast until they turn a rich brown and have an aromatic smell. It is not necessary to roast the chilli powder or spices.

Add laos and lemon rind to the ground spices. Parch the cloves, cinnamon stick, cardamom pods and mace in a dry pan over low heat, shaking the pan. Separate the cinnamon into layers, it will roast more quickly. Grind all the spices in mortar and pestle to a fine powder and combine with the previously roasted and ground ingredients. Set aside.

Heat oil in a frying pan and on low heat fry sliced onions and garlic until soft and golden brown, stirring occasionally. Add dried shrimp paste and fry for a minute longer, crushing it in the oil with back of spoon. Put this fried mixture, when it has cooled slightly, into container of electric blender with lemon rind and blend to a paste. If necessary, add a little coconut milk or water to assist action of blender. Turn into a bowl and combine with dry ground spices. The curry paste is now ready to use.

If a blender is not available, crush the onions and garlic as much as possible after they are cooked, combine with the spices and use in the same way.

Fresh and dried herbs and spices used in making curries.

Electric blenders take over from the Asian grinding stone for much of the preparation of curry powders and pastes.

BURMESE CURRIES

The ingredients basic to all Burmese curries never vary — onion, garlic, ginger, chilli and turmeric. The chilli can be used in powder form, or whole dried chillies can be ground with the other ingredients, but chilli is used sparingly and may be omitted if a hot curry is not desired. There will still be lots of flavour.

The more onions used, the thicker the 'gravy'. To make a curry for four people using 750 g (1½ lb) of meat, fish or poultry, here is a well-balanced mixture: one large onion, two or three cloves of garlic, one teaspoon finely grated fresh ginger, half a teaspoon ground turmeric and quarter teaspoon chilli powder, and two or three tablespoons oil for frying. Light sesame oil is best for capturing the true Burmese flavour (animal fat of any sort is never used). If corn, peanut, sunflower or other vegetable oil is used, add a small amount of Chinese-style dark sesame oil for flavour in the proportions of a teaspoon of sesame oil to a tablespoon of vegetable oil.

Preparation of Basic Ingredients

There is only one way to cook these basic ingredients in order to achieve a mellow flavour in which no single ingredient predominates.

Grind to a purée the onion, garlic and ginger. In the absence of the Asian grinding stone, this is best done in an electric blender, first chopping the ingredients roughly. It will be necessary to stop the motor frequently and scrape down the sides of the blender container. Or, if using the smaller blender jars (a supplement to many machines), lift off and shake the jar to redistribute the contents. When puréed smoothly, mix in the turmeric and chilli powder.

Heat 3 tablespoons of oil in a saucepan until smoking hot. Be careful when putting in the ground ingredients, for the hot oil splutters violently. Reduce heat and stir well to mix ingredients with the oil. Cover pan and simmer the mixture, lifting lid frequently to stir and scrape the base of pan with a wooden spoon. This initial frying takes at least 15 minutes. If mixture fries too rapidly and begins to stick before the smell has mellowed and the onions become transparent, add a small quantity of water from time to time and stir well. When the water content of the onions has evaporated and the ingredients turn a rich red-brown colour with oil showing around the edges of the mass, the first stage of cooking, and the most important one, is complete.

There is a Burmese term to describe this — see *byan*, meaning 'oil returned', that is, with the water completely evaporated and the oil returned to just oil. The basic ingredients will not have the required flavour unless this procedure is followed. The meat, fish or vegetables added will release their own juices while cooking slowly in the pan with the lid on. A roasting chicken will be sufficiently cooked by the time its own juices have evaporated. Boiling fowls, duck, some cuts of beef and pork may need a little water added from time to time as cooking continues until they are tender. Fish and prawns cook very quickly but some types may need a little more liquid added — fish stock, water or coconut milk. Vegetables seldom require any added liquid, but if a wetter result is preferred add water or coconut milk.

RICE, BREAD and noodles

In any country where curries are eaten daily, you will find that rice or noodles or many varieties of bread form the main part of the diet.

So great are the varieties of bread, and ways of cooking rice, that these recipes are only sampling of a subject that could fill a book on its own. However, included in this section are recipes that are representative of each of the curry-eating countries.

Three or four times as much rice or bread should be eaten with the curried meat, fish or poultry. In this way no digestive problems will be experienced. For the Westerner this a different but essential concept to grasp, when he has been used to considering meat, fish o poultry the main part of the meal.

While rice cooked in coconut milk or spicy stock is very nice for special occasions, perfectly cooked plain white rice or unpolished rice is served most often and really best combines with curries. Learn to cook rice by the absorption method as outlined in the recip that follow. You will soon appreciate why so many millions in Asia think of rice as the mos important food item and why, when asking if you have dined, the question, literally translated is: 'Have you eaten rice?'

STEAMED RICE

There are as many ways of cooking rice as there are cooks. Some wash the rice several times, others believe that valuable nutrients are lost in washing. Use your discretion — some imported rice really needs washing — but drain it well so the proportion of water to rice is retained. **Charmaine**

Serves: 6

500 g (1 lb) long grain rice
4 cups (32 fl oz) water
2½ teaspoons salt, optional

Use a saucepan with a well fitting lid. If using a stainless steel pan of the type where the lid forms a seal, reduce water by ¼ cup (2 fl oz).

Put rice, water and salt into pan and bring to the boil. As soon as it comes to the boil turn heat very low, cover tightly and allow to cook for 20 minutes. The liquid should be completely absorbed and the rice cooked perfectly. Uncover and allow steam to escape for a few minutes, then fluff rice with a fork and serve up using a metal spoon, for a wooden spoon would crush the grains.

Short Grain Rice: If cooking short grain rice, remember that the absorption rate is not as great as that of long grain rice. For 500 g (1 lb) rice, allow 2½ cups (20 fl oz) water for a very firm result, or 3 cups (24 fl oz) water for rice that is slightly softer but with each grain separate and not mushy.

Unpolished or Natural Rice: Rice that has not had its outer layer of bran removed is more nutritious as it is rich in Vitamin B. It does, however, take longer to cook. Use the same measurement as for long grain rice, or if a more tender result is preferred, add an extra ½ cup water. Cook in the same way, on very low heat, for 40-45 minutes.

Note: A most important point when cooking rice is that the lid should not be lifted during cooking time, for steam is lost and can affect the cooking time and the final result. Also, rice is never stirred during cooking. If rice needs washing, allow to drain in colander before starting to cook, or the measurement of water will not be accurate. Some cooks prefer to bring the water to the boil and then add the rice, but I find that either way the results are perfect as long as the measurements of rice and water are accurate and the rules for gentle steaming in a tightly covered pan are observed.

STEAMED RICE

Serves: 6

2½ cups (20 oz) long grain rice
2 teaspoons ghee
4 cups (32 fl oz) hot water
2½ teaspoons salt

Wash rice well if necessary. Drain in colander for 30 minutes. Heat ghee in a heavy-based saucepan with a well-fitting lid. Add rice and fry, stirring for about 2 minutes. Add hot water and salt, stir and bring quickly to the boil. Turn heat very low, cover tightly and cook, without lifting lid or stirring, for 20-25 minutes. Uncover to allow steam to escape for a minute or two, then lightly fluff up rice with fork, taking care not to mash the grains, which will be firm and separate and perfectly cooked. Dish up using a slotted metal spoon rather than a wooden spoon, which will crush the grains. Serve with curries or other spiced dishes.

SRI LANKA
YELLOW RICE
(Picture page 110)

This is so rich and full of flavour that it is served only on special occasions. **Reuben.**

Serves: 6

500 g (1 lb) long grain rice
4 tablespoons ghee
2 medium onions, finely sliced
6 cloves
20 black peppercorns
12 cardamom pods, bruised
1½ teaspoons ground turmeric
3½ teaspoons salt
12 curry leaves
1 stem lemon grass, optional
4 pieces daun pandan or rampé leaf, optional
about 4 cups (32 fl oz) coconut milk

Wash rice and drain thoroughly. Heat ghee in a large saucepan, add onion and fry until it begins to turn golden brown. Add cloves, peppercorns, cardamom pods, turmeric, salt, curry leaves, lemon grass and pandan or rampé leaf. Add rice and fry, stirring constantly, for 2-3 minutes, until rice is well coated with ghee and turmeric. Add coconut milk and bring to the boil. Reduce heat, cover and cook for 20-25 minutes without lifting lid.

When rice is cooked, the spices will have come to the top. Remove spices and leaves used for flavouring and fluff up the rice lightly with a fork. Serve hot, with curries and accompaniments.

INDIA
SAVOURY RICE & LENTILS

A good one-dish meal and often the basis of a vegetarian menu as the lentils provide protein. **Charmaine.**

Serves: 4-6

1 cup (8 oz) long grain rice
1 cup (6 oz) red lentils
2½ tablespoons ghee
2 medium onions, finely sliced
3½ cups (28 fl oz) hot water
2½ teaspoons salt
1½ teaspoons garam masala (see page 14)

Wash rice and drain well. Wash lentils well, removing any that float to the surface, then drain thoroughly.

Heat ghee in a saucepan and fry onion gently until golden brown. Remove half the onion and reserve. Add rice and lentils to pan and fry, stirring constantly, for about 3 minutes. Add hot water, salt and garam masala. Bring to the boil, cover and simmer over very low heat for 20-25 minutes or until rice and lentils are cooked. Do not lift the lid or stir during cooking time. Serve hot, garnished with reserved fried onion, and accompanied by curries.

Note: Whole spices, i.e. small cinnamon stick and a few whole cloves, cardamoms and peppercorns may be used instead of garam masala.

BURMA
RICE NOODLES WITH CURRY

This Burmese curry is almost like a soup and makes a simple, delicious meal. **Charmaine.**

Serves: 6-8

1 x 1.5 kg (3 lb) roasting chicken
1 teaspoon ground turmeric
2 teaspoons salt
¼ cup (2 fl oz) fish sauce
1½ cups (12 fl oz) thick coconut milk
3 large onions, finely sliced
1½ teaspoons finely chopped garlic
½ cup (2 oz) besan
2 cups (16 fl oz) thin coconut milk
4 eggs, hard-boiled
500 g (1 lb) rice noodles, dried *or* 1 kg
   (2 lb) fresh rice noodles
2 teaspoons chilli oil (see Glossary)

Joint chicken and put into a saucepan with turmeric, salt, fish sauce and just enough water to almost cover. Bring to the boil then reduce heat, cover and simmer until chicken is tender. Cool, then discard bones and cut meat into small pieces.

Cook thick coconut milk in a saucepan, stirring constantly, until it becomes thick and oil rises to the top. Keep cooking until it is very oily, then add the onions and garlic and fry, stirring, until they start to colour.

Add chicken meat to the frying onions and cook, stirring constantly for a few minutes. Set aside.

Mix besan with cold water to form a thin cream. Add thin coconut milk to the pan and when it comes to the boil stir in the besan mixture. Cook and stir constantly until it thickens, taking care it does not become lumpy or stick at the base of the pan. Add strained chicken stock a little at a time until the gravy is as thick as that of a stew. Add the chicken and onion mixture.

If fresh rice noodles are bought as large sheets, cut them into narrow strips and pour boiling water over them in a colander or steam gently for a few minutes to heat through.

Bring the chicken combination to simmering point, stir in chilli oil and remove from the heat. Serve in a large bowl, with noodles, sliced hard-boiled eggs and raw onions served separately.

Note: If dried rice noodles are used, they will have to be soaked 2 hours in cold water, then drained and boiled in a large amount of water until cooked through. Do not overcook and drain well.

MALAYSIA
COCONUT RICE

Serves: 4-5

500 g (1 lb) medium or long grain rice
1¼ cups (10 fl oz) coconut milk
2½ teaspoons salt

Soak rice in cold water overnight. Drain rice, spread in top part of a steamer and steam over rapidly boiling water for 30 minutes. Halfway through steaming, stir rice and turn it so that the rice on the bottom comes to the top and vice versa.

Gently heat the coconut milk with the salt in a large saucepan, stirring. Do not boil. Add the steamed rice, stir well, cover tightly and let stand for a further 30 minutes, by which time the milk should be completely absorbed. Once more spread the rice in top of steamer, bring water back to the boil and steam for 30 minutes, starting on high heat and gradually turning heat lower until in the end the water merely simmers. Serve hot with meat, poultry, fish or vegetable dishes.

SRI LANKA
GHEE RICE

Very rich, very spicy, very, very tasty. **Reuben.**

Serves: 4-5

500 g (1 lb) Basmati *or* other long grain rice
2½ tablespoons ghee
1 large onion, finely sliced
4 whole cloves
6 cardamom pods, bruised
1 cinnamon stick
4 cups (32 fl oz) beef, chicken *or* mutton stock,
   or water and stock cubes
2½ teaspoons salt

Wash rice well and drain for at least 30 minutes. Heat ghee in a saucepan and fry onion until golden, add spices and drained rice. Fry, stirring with slotted metal spoon, for 5 minutes over a moderate heat. Add hot stock and salt and bring to the boil.

Reduce heat to very low, cover pan tightly with lid and cook for 15-20 minutes without lifting lid. At end of cooking time, uncover and allow steam to escape for 5 minutes. Gently fluff up rice with a fork, removing whole spices.

When transferring rice to a serving dish, again use a slotted metal spoon to avoid crushing grains of rice. Serve hot, accompanied by curries of meat and vegetables, pickles and sambols.

MALAYSIA
GLUTINOUS YELLOW RICE

Don't expect this rice to be light and fluffy — the sticky consistency is how Malaysians like it. **Charmaine.**

Serves: 6

500 g (1 lb) glutinous rice
2 cups (16 fl oz) water
2 teaspoons salt
1 clove garlic, crushed
1 teaspoon ground turmeric
½ teaspoon ground black pepper
1 daun pandan
2 cups (16 fl oz) hot coconut milk

Garnish
crisp fried onion flakes

Wash rice and drain. Put into a saucepan with water, salt, garlic, turmeric, pepper and pandanus leaf for flavouring. Bring to the boil, reduce heat, cover tightly and steam for 10 minutes.

Uncover, add coconut milk (which should be very hot), and with a long-pronged fork stir gently so that the rice is mixed with the coconut milk. Cover and cook 10 minutes longer. Serve garnished with onion flakes and accompanied by curries and other dishes.

THAILAND
THAI FRIED RICE

Serve this by itself as a snack, or with curry as a meal. **Charmaine.**

Serves: 4

4 cups (1½ lb) cold cooked rice
3 tablespoons peanut oil
2 medium onions, finely chopped
1 large pork chop, finely diced
250 g (8 oz) raw prawns, shelled and de-veined
185 g (6 oz) crab meat
3 eggs, beaten
salt and pepper to taste
2 tablespoons fish sauce
1 tablespoon chilli sauce, optional
2 tablespoons tomato paste
1 cup (4 oz) chopped spring onions
3 tablespoons chopped fresh coriander leaves

Cook rice, spread out and allow to cool. Heat oil in a wok or large frying pan and fry the onions on medium low heat, stirring constantly, until soft and translucent. Increase heat to high. Add pork and fry for 3 minutes. Add prawns and crab meat and fry for a further 3 minutes or until cooked.

Season beaten eggs well with salt and pepper and pour into centre of wok. Stir until just beginning to set, then add rice and stir well. Continue tossing and stirring until rice is heated through. Sprinkle fish sauce over and mix well, then add chilli sauce and tomato paste and toss thoroughly so the rice has a reddish colour. Remove from heat, stir the spring onions through, and transfer to serving platter. Sprinkle with chopped coriander leaves and serve.

BURMA
OIL RICE

Serves: 4-6

2 cups (16 oz) glutinous rice
3 large onions
1½ teaspoons turmeric
6 tablespoons oil
4 cups (32 fl oz) hot water
2 teaspoons salt
4 tablespoons toasted sesame seeds

Wash rice well and leave to drain and dry. Slice onions thinly, keeping them uniform in thickness. Sprinkle turmeric over onions and mix lightly. Heat oil in a medium-size saucepan and fry onions until brown. Remove two-thirds of the onions and set aside for garnish. Add rice to pan and stir until it is well mixed with the oil. Add water and salt, stir well and bring to the boil. Turn heat very low, cover tightly and cook for 20 minutes by which time the rice should be cooked and the water completely absorbed.

Serve hot, garnished with fried onion and accompanied by the sesame seed lightly bruised and mixed with a little salt.

Note: Some people like a crust on the rice. To encourage a crust to form leave the rice on low heat for 5-10 minutes longer until a slight crackling sound is heard.

INDIA
RICE COOKED IN STOCK WITH SPICES

This classic pilau goes best with North Indian curries like Lamb Korma or Hundred Almond Curry. **Charmaine.**

Serves: 4-6

1 x 1 kg (2 lb) chicken *or* 3 lamb shanks
4 cardamom pods
10 whole black peppercorns
4½ teaspoons salt
1 onion
3 whole cloves
2½ cups (20 oz) long grain rice
5 tablespoons ghee
1 large onion, finely sliced
¼ teaspoon saffron strands *or*
   ⅛ teaspoon powdered saffron
2 cloves garlic, crushed
½ teaspoon finely grated fresh ginger
½ teaspoon garam masala (see page 1 4)
½ teaspoon ground cardamom
3 tablespoons rose water
¼ cup (1½ oz) sultanas

Garnish
¼ cup (1 oz) fried almonds
1 cup (6 oz) hot cooked green peas
3 hard-boiled eggs, halved

Make a strong, well-flavoured stock by simmering chicken or lamb in water to cover, with cardamom pods, peppercorns, 2 teaspoons salt and the onion stuck with cloves. Simmer for approximately 2 hours. Cool slightly, strain stock and measure 4 cups. Remove meat from bones, cut into bite-size pieces and set aside.

Wash rice thoroughly in water, drain in a colander and allow to dry for at least 1 hour. Heat ghee in a large saucepan and fry sliced onion until golden. Add saffron, garlic and ginger and fry for 1 minute, stirring constantly. Add rice and fry 5 minutes longer over a moderate heat, stirring with a slotted metal spoon. (This prevents breaking the long delicate grains of rice which add so much to the appearance of this dish.) Add hot stock, garam masala, cardamom, remaining salt, rose water, sultanas and reserved chicken pieces, and stir well. Cover pan with a tightly fitting lid and cook over a very low heat for 20 minutes. Do not uncover saucepan or stir rice during cooking time.

When rice is cooked, remove from heat, and leave uncovered for 5 minutes. Fluff up rice gently with a fork and place in a dish, again using a slotted metal spoon. Garnish with almonds, peas and eggs and serve hot accompanied by an Indian curry, pickles, sliced cucumbers in sour cream or yoghurt, and crisp fried pappadams.

INDONESIA
RICE COOKED IN COCONUT MILK WITH SPICES

Serves: 6

500 g (1 lb) long grain rice
4½ cups (36 fl oz) coconut milk
2½ teaspoons salt
1 onion, finely chopped
1 teaspoon finely chopped garlic
1 teaspoon ground turmeric
1 teaspoon ground cummin
2 teaspoons ground coriander
½ teaspoon dried shrimp paste
¼ teaspoon kencur powder
1 teaspoon finely chopped lemon rind,
    or 1 stem of lemon grass, chopped

If rice needs washing, wash and drain well. Put all ingredients except rice into a saucepan with a well-fitting lid, and bring slowly to the boil, uncovered, stirring frequently.

Add the rice, stir and bring back to the boil. Turn heat as low as possible, cover pan tightly and steam for 20 minutes. Uncover, fork rice lightly from around sides of pan, mixing in any coconut milk that has not been absorbed, replace lid and steam for 5 minutes longer. Serve hot with Indonesian or Malaysian curries and accompaniments.

INDIA
CHAPATIS

Flat discs of unleavened bread, with a delightful flavour and chewy texture. Serve with the dry type of curries which can be scooped up on a piece of chapati. **Charmaine.**

Yield: 20-24

3 cups (12 oz) fine wholemeal flour *or* roti flour
1-1½ teaspoons salt, *or* to taste
1 tablespoon ghee *or* oil, optional
1 cup (8 fl oz) lukewarm water

Put flour in mixing bowl, reserving about half a cup for rolling chapatis. Mix salt through the flour in the bowl, then rub in ghee or oil, if used. Add water all at once and mix to a firm but not stiff dough. Knead dough for at least 10 minutes (the more it is kneaded, the lighter the bread will be). Form dough into a ball, cover with clear plastic wrap and stand for 1 hour or longer. (If left overnight the chapatis will be very light and tender.)

Shape dough into balls about the size of a large walnut. Roll out each one on a lightly floured board (using reserved flour) to a circular shape as thin as a French crepe. After rolling out chapatis, heat a griddle plate or heavy-based frying pan until very hot, and cook the chapatis, starting with those that were rolled first (the resting between rolling and cooking seems to make for lighter chapatis). Put chapati on griddle and leave for about 1 minute. Turn and cook other side a further minute, pressing lightly around the edges of the chapati with a folded tea towel or an egg slice. This encourages bubbles to form and makes the chapatis light. As each one is cooked, wrap in a clean tea towel until all are ready. Serve immediately with butter, dry curries or vegetable dishes.

Note: In India, the chapatis are cooked on the tawa or griddle and are held for a moment or two right over the fire. This makes them puff up like balloons. You can do this over a gas flame, holding them with kitchen tongs.

PURI (Deep-fried Wholemeal Bread)

Children love this crisp, wholemeal bread. **Charmaine.**

Proceed as for chapatis. When all the dough is rolled out heat approximately 2.5 cm (1 in) of oil in a deep frying pan. When a faint haze rises from the oil, fry puris one at a time, over a moderate heat. Spoon hot oil continually over the cooking puri until it puffs and swells. Turn over and fry other side in the same way. When both sides are pale golden brown, drain on absorbent paper. Serve immediately with curries.

Note: Puri is pronounced 'poo-ree'.

PARATHA (Flaky Wholemeal Bread)

This would have to be my favourite among the Indian breads and my thanks go to an old family friend who taught me this very easy method of achieving the numerous flaky layers that make parathas so special. **Charmaine.**

Makes: 12-14

1½ cups (6 oz) fine wholemeal flour
1½ cups (6 oz) plain white flour *or* roti flour
1½ teaspoons salt
6-8 tablespoons ghee
1 cup (8 fl oz) water
extra ghee for cooking

Sieve wholemeal flour, white flour and salt into a mixing bowl and rub in 1 tablespoon of the ghee. Add water, mix and knead dough as for chapatis. Cover dough with clear plastic and set aside for 1 hour.

Divide dough into 12-14 equal portions and roll each into a smooth ball. Melt ghee over a low heat and cool slightly. Roll each ball of dough on a lightly floured board into a very thin circular shape. Pour about 2 teaspoons of the melted ghee into the centre of each and spread lightly with the hand.

With a knife, make a cut from the centre of each circle to the outer edge. Starting at the cut edge, roll the dough closely into a cone shape. Pick it up, press the apex of the cone and the base towards each other and flatten slightly. You will now have a small, roughly circular lump of dough again. Lightly flour the board again and roll out the dough very gently, taking care not to press too hard so that the air does not escape at the edges. The parathas should be as round as possible, but not as thinly rolled as the first time — about the size of a breakfast plate.

Cook on a hot griddle liberally greased with extra ghee, turning parathas and spreading with more ghee, until they are golden brown. Serve hot with curries or grilled kebabs, sambals and fresh mint chutney, page 102.

Note: The wholemeal and plain or roti flour can be replaced by 3 cups plain white flour.

meat

Pork is widely used in Asia, for pigs are the cheapest animals to raise. Sheep and goats are used for mutton, and beef may come from buffaloes more often than from bulls.

While tender lamb, beef or pork is desirable for quickly cooked dishes like satays, kebabs and so on, for curries it is actually an advantage to use the cuts of meat which allow for longer cooking.

The longer and more slowly a curry is cooked, the more the flavours blend and mellow. If prepared a day or two (or even more) ahead of time, they actually improve. And each re-heating seems to make the curry taste better. Here is the best solution for using more economical cuts — curry them! An added bonus is that the economy meats like skirt or flank steak, shin or gravy beef, hogget, pork belly and so on, have more flavour than tender fillet and are therefore the best choice for cooking with robust spices. Your venture into curry cookery may also be a means of lowering the food budget.

Do remember, when cooking beef or mutton, to trim off all excess fat. Even pork, though essentially a fatty meat, should not be too fat if a meal is to be appreciated and not followed by that 'too rich' feeling which is so unwelcome. Always serve meat curries with a large proportion of rice or bread to offset the spiciness and absorb the richness.

Although to the average westerner, meat is the main part of the meal, prepared as curry it cannot be eaten in so large a quantity. There should be at least twice as much rice or bread to help it down. For a world that is looking at ways to reduce the consumption of meat, both for economic and health reasons, this may well be the solution!

SRI LANKA
BEEF SMOORE

Pot Roast glorified. And how!   **Reuben.**

Serves: 6-8

1.5 kg (3 lb) fresh silverside *or* other stewing steak,
   in one piece
2 medium onions, finely chopped
3 teaspoons finely chopped garlic
1 tablespoon finely chopped fresh ginger
1 stick cinnamon
10 curry leaves
1 stem fresh lemon grass *or* 2 strips lemon rind
3 tablespoons Ceylon curry powder (see page 17)
½ teaspoon fenugreek seeds
½ cup (4 fl oz) vinegar
½ pickled lime *or* lemon
   or ½ cup tamarind liquid
2 cups (16 fl oz) thin coconut milk
1 teaspoon ground turmeric
2 teaspoons chilli powder, *or* to taste
2 teaspoons salt, *or* to taste
1 cup (8 fl oz) thick coconut milk
2½ tablespoons ghee

Pierce the meat well with a skewer and put in a large
saucepan with all the ingredients except the thick
coconut milk and ghee. Cover and simmer gently until
meat is tender, approximately 1½-2 hours. Add thick
coconut milk and cook, uncovered for 15 minutes
longer.

   Lift meat out on to a serving dish and if gravy is too
thin, reduce by boiling rapidly uncovered. Transfer
gravy to a bowl. Rinse pan to remove any gravy, return
to stove and heat ghee in it. Fry meat on all sides, pour
gravy over meat and heat through.

   To serve, cut meat into thick slices and spoon gravy
over.

SRI LANKA
BEEF CURRY

(Picture page 110)

Serves: 8-10

1.5 kg (3 lb) stewing beef steak
3 tablespoons ghee *or* oil
2 large onions, finely chopped
1 tablespoon finely chopped fresh ginger
3 teaspoons finely chopped garlic
4 tablespoons Ceylon curry powder, page 17
1 teaspoon ground turmeric
2 teaspoons black mustard seeds
2 teaspoons salt
1 tablespoon vinegar
2 fresh red chillies, seeded and chopped
3 ripe tomatoes, peeled and chopped

Cut steak into 5 cm (2 in) squares. Heat ghee in
saucepan and gently fry onions, ginger and garlic until
just beginning to turn golden. Add curry powder, turmeric, mustard seeds and fry over low heat for 2-3
minutes. Add salt and vinegar and stir well. Add steak
and fry, stirring to coat meat well. Add chillies and
tomatoes, cover pan and simmer on very low heat for
about 2 hours. Serve with rice and other accompaniments. If gravy is too thin when meat is tender, cook
over high heat, uncovered, until reduced.

THAILAND
RED CURRY OF BEEF

(Picture page 1)

Dried makrud rind and citrus leaves give the distinctive lemony tang to this curry. **Charmaine.**

Serves: 6

1 kg (2 lb) stewing steak
2 cups (16 fl oz) thick coconut milk
3 tablespoons red curry paste (see page 18)
2 cups (16 fl oz) thin coconut milk
2 sprigs tender citrus leaves
1 tablespoon dried makrud rind, soaked
1 teaspoon salt
2 tablespoons fish sauce
2 fresh red chillies, seeded and sliced

Trim the meat and cut into cubes. Make coconut milk (see page 9) and leave the first extract or thick milk in the refrigerator long enough for the cream to rise to the top, then spoon it off until you have a cup of the top of the coconut milk. Simmer this in a large saucepan, stirring constantly, until it comes to the boil, then cook over a low heat until the cream thickens and the oil starts to show around the edges. Add the curry paste and fry for 5 minutes or so, stirring constantly.

When done, the curry paste will smell fragrant and mellow, and oil will start to separate from the mass again. Add beef and stir well, then add remaining coconut milk, both first and second extracts. Add all remaining ingredients. Stir while bringing to the boil, then lower heat and simmer uncovered until beef is tender. If the beef has not become tender and the gravy seems to be cooking away, add a little more coconut milk or hot water and stir. The gravy should be rich and red, and there should be quite a lot of it. Serve with white rice and side dishes.

SRI LANKA
BEEF PEPPER CURRY

When in Colombo, this dish has priority in my selection of Sri Lankan curries. **Reuben.**

Serves: 8

1 kg (2 lb) lean stewing steak
2 teaspoons salt
2-4 teaspoons ground black pepper
1 tablespoon ground coriander
2 teaspoons ground cummin
1 teaspoon ground fennel
½ teaspoon ground turmeric
2 medium onions, finely chopped
1½ teaspoons finely chopped garlic
1½ teaspoons finely grated fresh ginger
2 fresh red chillies, seeded and sliced
8 curry leaves
2 strips daun pandan (rampé leaf)
1 stem fresh lemon grass *or* 2 strips lemon rind
2 tablespoons vinegar
2 cups (16 fl oz) thin coconut milk
1 tablespoon ghee *or* oil
1 cup (8 fl oz) thick coconut milk

Cut the meat into 5 cm (2 in) squares and beat lightly with a meat mallet. Season with salt and pepper and mix well. Roast separately in a dry pan the coriander, cummin and fennel. Add coriander to meat and set aside the cummin and fennel. Put meat into a saucepan with spices and all other ingredients except roasted cummin, fennel, ghee and the thick coconut milk.

Bring slowly to the boil, reduce heat and simmer covered, until meat is tender. If gravy thickens too quickly add a little water. Pour gravy into another pan, and to the meat left in the pan add the ghee or oil and let the meat fry in it for a few minutes, stirring. Add the cummin and fennel to the thick coconut milk and mix with the cooked gravy, then return everything to pan with the meat and continue to simmer uncovered over a very low heat until the gravy is thick and the various flavours are well blended. Serve with rice and other accompaniments.

BURMA

BEEF CURRY, VERY DRY

Serves: 4-6

750 g (1½ lb) stewing steak
2 large onions
5 large cloves garlic
2 teaspoons chopped fresh ginger
1 teaspoon ground turmeric
1 teaspoon chilli powder
6 tablespoons light sesame oil *or* corn oil
¼ teaspoon ground black pepper
2 tender stems lemon grass, finely sliced, *or*
　4 strips lemon rind
1 cup (8 fl oz) hot water
1½ teaspoons salt

Garnish
2 large onions, finely sliced and fried
　until crisp and brown

Cut beef into 5 cm (2 in) squares. Cook basic ingredients as described on page 21. When well cooked and sizzling, add beef, pepper and lemon grass or rind. Continue frying and stirring until all juices from the beef have completely evaporated and meat changes colour.

Add water and salt, cover and simmer until meat is tender, adding more water if necessary. Remove lid, raise heat and cook rapidly until the meat is oily-dry and well coated with the gravy. Garnish with fried onions and serve with white rice and accompaniments.

INDIA

MEAT & POTATO CURRY

(Picture on opposite page)

A good recipe when watching the budget. Less meat, more potatoes, and still delicious. **Charmaine.**

Serves: 6-8

1.5 kg (3 lb) hogget *or* beef
¼ cup (2 fl oz) oil *or* 2 tablespoons ghee
1 teaspoon black mustard seeds
½ teaspoon fenugreek seeds
3 teaspoons finely chopped garlic
1 tablespoon finely chopped fresh ginger
3 medium onions, finely sliced
1½ teaspoons ground turmeric
2 tablespoons ground coriander
1 tablespoon ground cummin
2 teaspoons chilli powder
3 teaspoons salt
2 tablespoons vinegar
2 teaspoons garam masala (see page 1 4)
2 tablespoons extra vinegar
750 g (1½ lb) potatoes, peeled and cubed
2 tablespoons chopped fresh coriander leaves,
　optional

Trim steak of fat and gristle and cut into small cubes. Heat oil in a large saucepan and fry the mustard seeds until they pop. Add fenugreek seeds, garlic, ginger and onion and fry over medium heat, stirring occasionally with a wooden spoon, until onions just begin to brown. Add turmeric and fry for a minute longer. Add coriander, cummin and chilli powder and stir for a minute or so, then add salt and vinegar and stir until liquid dries up. Sprinkle in the garam masala and mix well. Add the cubed meat, stirring so that all the pieces are coated with the spice mixture. If there is much of the spice sticking to the base of the pan, add the extra vinegar and stir, scraping as much as possible from the base of the pan.

Reduce heat, cover with well-fitting lid and let meat and spice mixture simmer for 1½-2 hours or until meat is tender. Depending on the type of meat used, it may be necessary to add a little water. Add the cubed potatoes, cover once more and cook for 20-25 minutes or until done. Sprinkle with fresh coriander leaves and serve hot with rice or Indian bread.

Red Prawn Curry, recipe page 67; Meat and Potato Curry, recipe on opposite page.

Kofta Curry, recipe on opposite page.

NORTH INDIA
KOFTA CURRY

(Picture on opposite page)

You'll never dream minced meat can taste so good. **Charmaine.**

Serves: 6

Koftas:
750 g (1½ lb) finely minced lamb
1 medium onion, finely chopped
½ teaspoon crushed garlic
½ teaspoon finely grated fresh ginger
1 red *or* green fresh chilli, seeded and finely chopped
3 tablespoons chopped fresh coriander *or* mint
1½ teaspoons salt
1 teaspoon garam masala (see page 14)

Gravy:
3 tablespoons ghee *or* oil
2 medium onions, finely chopped
1 teaspoon finely chopped garlic
1 tablespoon finely chopped fresh ginger
1 teaspoon ground turmeric
1 teaspoon garam masala
1 teaspoon chilli powder
2 ripe tomatoes, peeled and chopped
1 teaspoon salt
2 tablespoons chopped coriander *or* mint
lemon juice to taste

Koftas: Mix minced lamb thoroughly with all the other ingredients. Shape into small balls.

Gravy: Heat ghee in a large, heavy saucepan, brown the koftas, remove from pan and set aside. In the same pan fry the onion, garlic and ginger until soft and golden. Add turmeric, garam masala and chilli powder, fry for 1 minute. Add tomato, salt and koftas, cover and simmer for 25 minutes or until gravy is thick and koftas tender. Stir in chopped herbs and lemon juice. Serve with rice or chapatis and various accompaniments.

INDIA
BEEF & CARDAMOM CURRY

A fairly strong flavour of cardamom distinguishes this curry. **Reuben.**

Serves: 4

500 g (1 lb) lean stewing steak
2 tablespoons peanut oil
1 large onion, sliced
1 teaspoon finely chopped garlic
1 teaspoon finely chopped fresh ginger
½ teaspoon turmeric
2 teaspoons ground cardamom
1 teaspoon ground coriander
1 teaspoon ground cummin
1 x 5 cm (2 in) cinnamon stick
pinch of ground cloves
1 teaspoon chilli powder
1 tablespoon lemon juice
6 curry leaves
salt to taste
½ cup (4 fl oz) warm water

Cut meat into 5 cm (2 in) squares. Heat oil in a saucepan, add onions and fry, stirring occasionally, until golden brown. Add meat, raise heat and brown all over. Add all other ingredients except the water, mix with the meat and cook for 3 minutes.

Add water, lower heat, cover and simmer till meat is tender, adding more water if necessary. Stir occasionally to prevent meat sticking to base of saucepan. Serve with boiled rice and accompaniments.

INDONESIA

JAVANESE MINCED STEAK CURRY

Very popular with the junior set, and you can leave out the chilli powder if you (or they) prefer.   **Charmaine.**

Serves: 4

500 g (1 lb) minced steak
1 medium onion, roughly chopped
1 teaspoon chopped garlic
1 teaspoon laos
1 teaspoon ground coriander
1 teaspoon shrimp paste
¼ cup (1 oz) roasted peanuts
¼ teaspoon ground black pepper
1 teaspoon chilli powder
¼ cup (2 fl oz) warm water
1 tablespoon peanut oil
1 stem lemon grass
   or chopped rind of ½ lemon
1 teaspoon salt
¼ cup thick coconut milk

Into container of electric blender put onion, garlic, laos, coriander, shrimp paste, peanuts, pepper and chilli powder. Blend to a paste adding a little water to facilitate blending.

Heat oil in a saucepan, stir in the contents of blender jar, add lemon grass or lemon rind and fry for 5 minutes. Sprinkle in 1 teaspoon salt, stir, cover and simmer for 30 minutes. Add the coconut milk and cook uncovered for a further 10 minutes, stirring frequently. Serve with hot boiled rice, fried prawn crisps or other side dishes.

THAILAND

MOSLEM BEEF CURRY

Serves: 6-8

1 kg (2 lb) stewing beef
2 tablespoons peanut oil
2 teaspoons finely chopped garlic
1 large onion, sliced
2 tablespoons Moslem curry paste (see page 18)
2 tablespoons basil leaves *or*
   2 teaspoons dried basil
1 teaspoon chilli powder
2 teaspoons sugar
5 cm (2 in) cinnamon stick
2 teaspoons salt
1 cup (8 fl oz) warm water
4 tablespoons thick coconut milk

Garnish
½ cup (2 oz) chopped, roasted peanuts

Cut beef into 2.5 cm (1 in) squares. Heat oil in a saucepan and add garlic and sliced onion and fry till golden brown. Add meat and brown on high heat, stirring frequently.

Stir in the curry paste, basil leaves, chilli powder, sugar, cinnamon and salt. Add water and bring to the boil, cover and simmer till meat is tender and oil comes to the surface. Stir in the coconut milk, simmer 2 minutes longer uncovered and serve garnished with chopped peanuts.

MALAYSIA
SATAY CURRY

While meat marinates, prepare gravy, or if more convenient, prepare gravy a day or two before — it improves the flavour. Grill satays just before serving.

Serves: 4-6

Satays:
750 g (1½ lb) grilling steak
1 medium onion, roughly chopped
1 teaspoon chopped garlic
1 teaspoon chopped fresh ginger
1½ teaspoons salt
½ teaspoon ground black pepper
1 stem fresh lemon grass, finely sliced *or*
    rind of half a lemon, chopped
½ teaspoon ground fennel
4 candle nuts *or* 3 brazil kernels, chopped
4 dried red chillies
½ teaspoon dried shrimp paste

Curry Gravy:
1 medium onion, roughly chopped
1 teaspoon chopped garlic
1 teaspoon chopped fresh ginger
1 stem fresh lemon grass, chopped *or*
    rind of half a lemon, chopped
2 teaspoons ground coriander
1 teaspoon ground cummin
½ teaspoon ground cinnamon
½ teaspoon ground cloves
½ teaspoon ground cardamom
4 candle nuts *or* 3 brazil kernels, chopped
1 teaspoon dried shrimp paste
4 dried red chillies
1 teaspoon salt
½ teaspoon ground black pepper
3 tablespoons peanut oil
1 cup (8 fl oz) coconut milk

Satays: Cube grilling steak and set aside in a bowl. Place rest of ingredients in container of electric blender and blend to a smooth paste, adding a little water to facilitate blending. Marinate meat in this mixture for at least 30 minutes. Thread pieces of meat on small bamboo skewers and grill until well done, turning skewers so meat cooks on all sides. Place on a dish, pour the gravy over satays and serve with rice and accompaniments such as sliced cucumber and onion, or Malay pickles (see page 112).

Curry Gravy: Place all ingredients, excepting coconut milk and peanut oil, in container of electric blender and blend to a smooth paste, adding a little water to facilitate blending.

Heat oil in a saucepan, stir in blended mixture and cook until it smells aromatic. Add the coconut milk and cook, stirring occasionally, until it thickens and the oil comes to the surface. Pour this gravy over the satays.

NORTH INDIA
MINCED MEAT & POTATO CURRY

Good as a filling for curry puffs too! **Charmaine.**

Serves: 4-6

3 tablespoons oil *or* ghee
2 medium onions, finely chopped
1 teaspoon finely chopped garlic
1 teaspoon finely grated fresh ginger
½ teaspoon ground turmeric
2 teaspoons ground coriander
1 teaspoon ground cummin
½ teaspoon chilli powder, optional
2 teaspoons salt
2 tablespoons lemon juice *or* vinegar
500 g (1 lb) minced lamb *or* beef
500 g (1 lb) potatoes, peeled and quartered
1 cup (8 fl oz) hot water
1 teaspoon garam masala (see page 14)

Garnish
2 tablespoons chopped fresh mint *or* coriander

Heat oil in a heavy saucepan and fry the onions, garlic and ginger until soft and golden. Add turmeric, coriander, cummin and chilli powder and fry, stirring, for 1 minute. Add the salt and lemon juice and when it starts to sizzle fry the meat, stirring constantly, until all the meat is browned and any lumps broken up.

Add the potatoes and hot water, bring to simmering point, cover and cook on low heat until potatoes are done and meat tender, about 30 minutes. Stir occasionally towards end of this time to ensure curry does not stick on base of pan. Sprinkle the garam masala over, stir gently, then garnish with the chopped herbs. Serve with rice or Indian breads.

MALAYSIA

BEEF & TOASTED COCONUT CURRY

The toasted coconut makes for quite an unusual curry. At the food stall in Kuala Lumpur they stepped up the chillies, garlic and blachan. **Reuben**

Serves: 4-6

1 kg (2 lb) lean stewing steak, thinly sliced
3 tablespoons peanut oil
3 tablespoons desiccated coconut
1 stem lemon grass, chopped or
  rind of half lemon
4 dried red chillies
1 teaspoon chopped garlic
1 teaspoon chopped fresh ginger
1 medium onion, roughly chopped
1 teaspoon dried shrimp paste
4 tablespoons tamarind liquid, page 122
2 teaspoons salt

Roast coconut in a dry pan till golden brown. Remove to a plate and when cool put into blender container together with rest of ingredients and blend to a smooth paste adding a little hot water to facilitate blending.

Heat oil in a saucepan then add blended spices and cook, stirring till oil comes to the surface and spices smell aromatic. Add meat and stir till colour changes, then cover and simmer till meat is tender, stirring occasionally. Add more water if necessary.

Serve with rice and accompaniments.

INDONESIA

SUMATRAN BEEF CURRY

Serves: 4-6

1 kg (2 lb) lean stewing steak
1 large onion, roughly chopped
2 teaspoons chopped garlic
2 teaspoons ground coriander
2 teaspoons ground cummin
2 teaspoons dried shrimp paste
6 candle nuts or 4 Brazil nuts, chopped
8 dried red chillies
1 teaspoon laos powder
1 teaspoon ground turmeric
2 teaspoons salt
½ teaspoon ground black pepper
3 tablespoons peanut oil
1 cup (8 fl oz) coconut milk
4 tablespoons tamarind liquid, page 122

Cube the steak and set aside in a bowl. Place onion, garlic, coriander, cummin, shrimp paste, nuts, chillies, laos, turmeric, salt and pepper in container of electric blender and blend to a smooth paste, adding a little water to facilitate blending. Marinate meat in this mixture for 30 minutes.

Heat oil in a saucepan, stir in meat and marinade and cook till meat changes colour. Cover and simmer on very low heat till meat is tender, stirring occasionally. Juices from the meat should provide sufficient liquid, but if necessary add a little water.

Add coconut milk and continue stirring till oil comes to the surface. Stir in tamarind liquid cook a few more minutes uncovered, and serve with rice and accompaniments.

BURMA
BEEF & POTATO CURRY

Budget-stretching, Burmese style. Sometimes pumpkin is used instead of potato. **Charmaine.**

Serves: 4-6

750 g (1½ lb) beef
375 g (12 oz) potatoes
2 large onions
5 large cloves garlic
2 teaspoons chopped fresh ginger
1 teaspoon chilli powder
8 tablespoons light sesame oil *or* corn oil
½ teaspoon ground cummin
½ teaspoon ground coriander
1½ teaspoons salt *or* to taste
2 cups (16 fl oz) water

Cut beef into large squares. Peel and cut potatoes into quarters. Cook basic ingredients as described on page 21. When cooked and sizzling, add cummin and coriander, then add meat and fry, stirring for a few minutes. Add salt, about 2 cups water, potatoes and simmer slowly until meat is tender and potatoes are cooked.

Note: Some cooks prefer to rub the cummin, coriander and salt into the beef before cooking. Care must be taken to fry on low heat so spices will not burn.

MALAYSIA
HOT BEEF CURRY

We enjoyed this particular dish in Penang, and this is exactly as we had it. **Charmaine and Reuben.**

Serves: 4

500 g (1 lb) stewing steak
5 red *or* green chillies
1 large onion, roughly chopped
1 teaspoon chopped garlic
1 teaspoon chopped fresh ginger
¼ cup (1 oz) roasted peanuts
½ teaspoon ground nutmeg
½ teaspoon ground black pepper
1 teaspoon salt
1 tablespoon lemon juice
1 cup (8 fl oz) warm water
2 tablespoons peanut oil
1 tablespoon light soy sauce
3 daun salam or curry leaves

Cut meat into 5 cm (2 in) squares. Into container of electric blender put chillies, onion, garlic, ginger, peanuts, nutmeg, black pepper, salt and lemon juice. Blend to a paste, adding a little warm water to facilitate blending.

Heat oil in a saucepan, add contents of blender and cook for 5 minutes, stirring occasionally. Add meat and cook for a further 5 minutes. Add soy sauce, daun salam and rest of warm water, stir well, cover and simmer until meat is tender and oil comes to the top. Stir occasionally to prevent meat sticking to base of saucepan. Adjust seasoning and serve with hot rice and a sambal.

SPICY MUTTON CURRY

You may be able to purchase dried candle nuts from specialty stores. If not, substitute Brazil nuts. **Reuben.**

Serves: 6

750 g (1½ lb) hogget or lamb
4 tablespoons desiccated coconut
¼ cup (2 fl oz) tamarind liquid, page 122
2 large onions, roughly chopped
2 teaspoons chopped garlic
1 tablespoon roughly chopped fresh ginger
2 teaspoons ground coriander
1 teaspoon each ground cummin and turmeric
½ teaspoon each ground cinnamon, fennel,
    nutmeg and black pepper
¼ teaspoon each ground cloves and cardamom
4 candle nuts
4-8 dried red chillies, *or* to taste
2 tablespoons peanut oil
2 ripe tomatoes, chopped
1½ cups (12 fl oz) coconut milk
1½ teaspoons salt
1 stem fresh lemon grass, finely sliced, *or*
    1 teaspoon finely chopped lemon rind

Cut meat into small cubes. Brown the coconut in a dry frying pan, stirring constantly over medium low heat for 4 or 5 minutes or until it is a rich golden-brown colour. Set aside. Pour quarter cup (2 fl oz) very hot water over a walnut-size piece of dried tamarind pulp and leave for 5 minutes. Squeeze the tamarind in the water to dissolve. Strain through a fine sieve.

In container of electric blender put the tamarind liquid and onions and blend to a smooth, thick liquid. Add garlic and ginger and blend again. Add the spices, candlenuts, dried chillies and, last of all, the toasted coconut. Blend until smooth and well combined.

Heat the oil in a large saucepan and fry the blended mixture for 5 minutes, stirring frequently at the beginning and constantly at the end. Add meat and fry for 3 minutes, stirring well so that each piece is coated with spices. Add tomato and fry for a further 3 minutes. Add coconut milk, salt and lemon grass and bring slowly to the boil. Reduce heat to very low and simmer, uncovered, until meat is tender, stirring now and then. This may take from 1½ to 2 hours. Serve with white rice.

SKEWERED MUTTON CURRY

Charmaine very sweetly asked me to test this recipe. I wondered why. Just watch out for skewered fingers! **Reuben.**

Serves: 4-6

1 kg (2 lb) lamb *or* hogget
thin slices of fresh young ginger root
3 tablespoons ghee *or* oil
1 large onion, finely chopped
1½ teaspoons finely chopped garlic
1 tablespoon ground coriander
2 teaspoons ground cummin
½ teaspoon ground fennel
½ teaspoon ground turmeric
½ teaspoon ground black pepper
2 teaspoons salt
1 ripe tomato, diced
2 green chillies, sliced
½ teaspoon ground cinnamon
½ teaspoon ground cardamom
¼ teaspoon ground cloves

Cut meat into small cubes and thread on thin bamboo skewers which have been cut in 10 cm (4 in) lengths, alternating each piece of meat with a thin slice of ginger. Cut the ginger from a slender root so the slices will not be too big, or cut large slices in pieces.

Heat ghee or oil and fry onion over medium low heat until soft, stirring occasionally. Add garlic, stir and fry until onion is golden brown. Add coriander, cummin, fennel, turmeric and pepper and fry for 1 minute, then add salt and tomato and stir for 3 minutes longer. Add chillies and skewered meat and fry until meat is lightly brown. Turn heat low, cover and cook until meat is tender. Liquid from the meat will eventually be reabsorbed, leaving the gravy very thick. Stir occasionally to prevent spices catching on the base of the pan.

Ten minutes before end of cooking time sprinkle cinnamon, cardamom and cloves over the curry. Stir well and leave on very low heat. Serve hot with rice and accompaniments.

INDIA
MADRAS MUTTON CURRY

I said more chillies. No, she said and won the toss. I still say more chillies. **Reuben.**

Serves: 6-8

1.5 kg (3 lb) lamb forequarter chops *or* other meat, cubed
3 tablespoons oil
10 curry leaves
3 medium onions, finely chopped
3 teaspoons chopped garlic
1 tablespoon finely chopped fresh ginger
1 teaspoon ground turmeric
3-4 teaspoons chilli powder, *or* to taste
3 teaspoons ground coriander
1 teaspoon ground cummin
2½ teaspoons salt
2 tablespoons vinegar
2 *or* 3 fresh green chillies, split halfway from tip
2 tablespoons desiccated coconut
1½ cups (12 fl oz) coconut milk

Cut chops in large pieces, keeping the bone in. Heat oil in a large heavy saucepan and fry the curry leaves until brown. Add onions, garlic and ginger and fry until soft and golden. Add turmeric and fry for a few seconds, then put in chilli powder, coriander and cummin and fry for 1 minute.

Add salt and vinegar and stir until liquid evaporates, then put in the meat and stir until it is coated with the spices. Add green chillies, lower heat, cover and cook until the meat is tender. Juices come from the meat and there should be no need to add water.

Meanwhile, roast the coconut in a dry pan until golden brown. Grind finely in electric blender and if necessary add ½ cup (4 fl oz) of the coconut milk to facilitate blending. Blend on high speed for 30 seconds. Add to the curry together with the rest of the coconut milk and simmer uncovered until gravy is thick. Serve with rice and accompaniments.

INDIA
LAMB KORMA

One of the classic dishes of India and well worth trying. **Charmaine.**

Serves: 6

1 kg (2 lb) boned leg of lamb
2 medium onions
1 tablespoon chopped fresh ginger
2 teaspoons chopped garlic
¼ cup (1 oz) raw cashews *or* blanched almonds
2-6 dried chillies, seeded
2 teaspoons ground coriander
1 teaspoon ground cummin
¼ teaspoon ground cinnamon
¼ teaspoon ground cardamom
¼ teaspoon ground cloves
½ teaspoon saffron strands *or* ¼ teaspoon powdered saffron
2 tablespoons boiling water
1 tablespoon ghee
2 tablespoons oil
2 teaspoons salt
½ cup (4 fl oz) natural yoghurt
2 tablespoons chopped fresh coriander leaves

Cut lamb into large cubes, trimming off excess fat if any. Peel onion, slice one finely and set aside. Chop other onion roughly and put into container of electric blender with ginger, garlic, cashews and chillies. Add ½ cup (4 fl oz) water to blender jar, cover and blend on high speed for a minute or until all ingredients are ground smoothly. Add all the ground spices and blend for a few seconds longer.

Put saffron strands into a small bowl, pour the boiling water over and allow to soak while starting to cook the masala (ground spice mixture).

Heat ghee and oil in a large saucepan and when hot put in the finely sliced onion and fry, stirring frequently with a wooden spoon, until soft and golden. Add the blended mixture and continue to fry, stirring constantly until the masala is well cooked and the oil starts to separate from the mixture. Wash out blender container with an extra ¼ cup (2 fl oz) water, add to pan together with salt and continue to stir and fry until the liquid dries up once more.

Add the meat and stir over medium heat until each piece is coated with the spice. Stir the saffron, crushing the strands against side of the bowl, then add to the pan. Stir to mix well. Add yoghurt and stir again until evenly mixed. Reduce heat to low, cover and cook at a gentle simmer for 1 hour or until meat is tender and gravy thick. Stir occasionally, taking care that the spice mixture does not stick to base of pan. When lamb is tender, sprinkle with fresh coriander leaves, replace lid and cook for 5 minutes longer. Serve hot with rice.

INDONESIA
DRY MEAT CURRY

This is the famous Indonesian combination of spices that results in two types of curry — one is Kalio, which has a very thick gravy. The other is Rendang, created when the cooking is allowed to continue until the consistency is almost dry and the oil separates from the gravy. For Kalio, stop cooking after adding the thick coconut milk and bringing to simmering point. **Charmaine.**

Serves: 8

1·5 kg (3 lb) beef *or* mutton
2 medium onions
2 cloves garlic
1 tablespoon chopped fresh ginger
3 tablespoons peanut oil
1 small stick cinnamon
4 *or* 5 whole cloves
3 teaspoons ground coriander
1 teaspoon ground cummin
1 teaspoon ground black pepper
1 teaspoon chilli powder, *or* to taste
½ teaspoon ground fennel
½ teaspoon ground kencur (aromatic ginger)
3 tablespoons desiccated coconut, toasted
4 cups (32 fl oz) thin coconut milk
2 teaspoons salt
¼ cup (2 fl oz) tamarind liquid
1 cup (8 fl oz) thick coconut milk

Cut meat into large cubes. Finely slice one onion and set aside. Roughly chop the other onion and put into container of electric blender with garlic and ginger. (If blender is not available, finely grate the onion, garlic and ginger.) Blend to a smooth purée, adding 2 tablespoons of the thin coconut milk if necessary. Put meat into a bowl, mix well with ground ingredients and set aside.

In a large saucepan heat the oil and fry sliced onion and whole spices, stirring occasionally, until onion is soft and starts to turn golden. Add meat and fry until meat changes colour. Add ground spices, coconut, thin coconut milk and salt. Stir while bringing to the boil and continue stirring for about 10 minutes. Simmer uncovered until meat is almost tender. Add tamarind liquid, stir well and simmer until liquid is almost dry. Add thick coconut milk, stirring constantly, and allow to simmer again until oil separates from gravy and curry is very dry.

SRI LANKA
FRIED PORK CURRY

(Picture page 74)

One of the most popular dishes in Sri Lanka, especially on festive occasions. **Charmaine.**

Serves: 6-8

1 kg (2 lb) pork belly *or* forequarter
3 tablespoons oil
10 curry leaves
¼ teaspoon fenugreek seeds, optional
2 medium onions, finely chopped
2 teaspoons finely chopped garlic
1½ teaspoons finely grated fresh ginger
3 tablespoons Ceylon curry powder (see page 17)
1-2 teaspoons chilli powder
2 teaspoons salt
1 tablespoon vinegar
1 tablespoon tamarind pulp dissolved in
   1½ cups (12 fl oz) hot water
5 cm (2 in) cinnamon stick
4 cardamom pods
1 cup (8 fl oz) thick coconut milk

Cut pork into large cubes. Heat oil in a large saucepan and fry curry leaves and fenugreek, if used, until they start to brown. Add onion and garlic and fry over a low heat until soft and golden. Add ginger, curry powder, chilli powder, salt, vinegar and pork. Fry on high heat, stirring thoroughly until meat is well coated with the spice mixture. Squeeze tamarind pulp in hot water, strain and discard seeds. Add tamarind liquid, cinnamon and cardamom, cover and cook on low heat until pork is tender, about 1 hour. Add coconut milk and cook 10 minutes or more, uncovered.

Pour gravy into another saucepan, return pork to heat and allow to fry in its own fat. (If pork is not fat enough, add 1 tablespoon of ghee or oil to pan.) When pork is nicely brown, return gravy to pan and cook, uncovered, until gravy is thick. Serve hot with boiled rice.

MALAYSIA
HOT PORK CURRY

I like this! I should be forgiven!   **Reuben.**

Serves: 4

500 g (1 lb) forequarter of pork, boned
1 medium onion, roughly chopped
4 dried red chillies
3 fresh red chillies
4 candle nuts *or* 3 Brazil nuts, chopped
1 teaspoon dried shrimp paste
1 stem fresh lemon grass, sliced, *or*
   rind of ½ lemon
1 teaspoon turmeric
4 tablespoons peanut oil
1 cup (8 fl oz) pork *or* chicken stock
1 teaspoon sugar
1 tablespoon vinegar
1 teaspoon salt
1 large onion, finely sliced
2 teaspoons chopped garlic
1 tablespoon chopped fresh ginger

Cut pork into cubes and set aside. Place chopped onion, dried and fresh chillies, nuts, shrimp paste, lemon grass and turmeric in blender container and blend to a paste, adding a little stock to facilitate blending. Heat 2 tablespoons oil in a saucepan and fry spice mixture for 3-4 minutes, add meat and stir-fry till browned all over. Stir in stock, sugar, vinegar and salt and simmer covered until pork is cooked and liquid almost absorbed.

In another saucepan, heat remaining oil and fry the sliced onion, garlic and ginger till soft and golden brown. Add this to saucepan containing pork, bring to the boil and serve with rice.

SOUTH INDIA
PORK VINDALOO

Vindaloo denotes a hot, sour preparation which preserves meat without refrigeration for a few days.

Serves: 6-8

1 kg (2 lb) pork
6-8 large dried red chillies
1 cup (8 fl oz) vinegar, preferably coconut vinegar
2 teaspoons chopped fresh ginger
4 teaspoons chopped garlic
2 teaspoons ground cummin
½ teaspoon ground black pepper
½ teaspoon ground cinnamon
½ teaspoon ground cardamom
¼ teaspoon ground cloves
¼ teaspoon ground nutmeg
2 teaspoons salt
2-3 tablespoons ghee *or* oil
2 medium onions, finely chopped
1 tablespoon brown sugar

Cut pork into cubes. Soak chillies in vinegar for 10 minutes. If available use coconut vinegar for authentic flavour, but any kind of vinegar may be substituted, diluting it if it is very strong. Put chillies and vinegar, ginger, garlic, all the ground spices and salt into container of electric blender and blend until chillies are finely ground. Pour this mixture over the pork in an earthenware bowl, cover and marinate for 2 hours.

Heat enough ghee or oil to cover base of an enamel or stainless steel saucepan. (This dish is cooked in earthenware pots in India and if one is available it would be an advantage.) Fry the onions on low heat until soft and golden, stirring frequently. Drain pork from the marinade and fry on medium high heat, stirring, until it changes colour. Pour in marinade, cover pan and simmer on low heat until pork is tender, about 1½ hours. Stir in sugar. Serve with plain white rice.

BURMA
PORK CURRY, DRY

I sneaked this one in, another of my favourites.
Reuben.

Serves: 4

500 g (1 lb) pork
1 large onion
3 cloves garlic
1 teaspoon finely grated fresh ginger
½ teaspoon chilli powder
½ teaspoon ground turmeric
3 tablespoons light sesame oil *or* corn oil
1 stem lemon grass *or* 2 strips lemon rind
2 tablespoons tamarind liquid
1 teaspoon salt
1 tablespoon fish sauce

Cut pork into 5 cm (2 in) pieces. Excess fat should be removed or the curry will be too rich, but some fat left on the meat is quite acceptable.

Purée and cook onion, garlic, ginger, chilli and turmeric as described on page 21. When well cooked, add pork and simmer gently in its own juice until tender. In electric blender purée chopped lemon grass or rind, tamarind juice, salt and fish sauce. Add to pan and stir well. Cook until all water has evaporated and the oil separates from the gravy.

The flavour of the curry can be varied by adding extra chilli powder for a hot curry, or stirring in a piece of hot Indian mango pickle, chopped fresh coriander leaves or chopped spring onions

SRI LANKA
PORK PADRE CURRY

I notice that in Sri Lankan cookery, whenever a curry has that 'secret' ingredient, arrack, it becomes a padré curry. Perhaps this was the padré's only opportunity to imbibe! Whisky may be used instead of arrack, a spirit distilled from coconut palms. **Charmaine.**

Serves: 6-8

1.5 kg (3 lb) pork forequarter, boned
1 tablespoon ground coriander
2 teaspoons ground cummin
1 teaspoon fennel seeds
2 large onions, sliced
2 teaspoons chopped fresh ginger
2 teaspoons chopped garlic
rind of half lemon
2 teaspoons chilli powder
12 curry leaves
1 stick of cinnamon
¼ cup (2 fl oz) whisky *or* arrack
1 tablespoon sugar
½ teaspoon pepper
3 teaspoons salt
2 cups (16 fl oz) thick coconut milk
¼ cup (2 fl oz) tamarind liquid or vinegar

Cube pork and set aside. Roast the coriander, cummin and fennel (or use a dark roasted Ceylon curry powder). Put spices into container of electric blender together with onions, ginger, garlic, lemon rind, chilli powder and curry leaves. Add a cup (8 fl oz) of water and blend to a smooth paste. Put blended mixture and pork into a saucepan and add one cup (8 fl oz) of the coconut milk, the cinnamon, pepper, salt and tamarind. Bring to the boil, cover and simmer for 50 minutes.

Add sugar and whisky and simmer until pork is tender. If more liquid is needed, add a little hot water. Towards end of cooking time add remaining coconut milk and simmer, uncovered, until thick. Serve with rice and accompaniments.

SRI LANKA
PORK CURRY

Serves: 8

1 kg (2 lb) pork belly
8-10 large dried chillies
1½ cups (12 fl oz) hot water
1 tablespoon tamarind pulp
½ teaspoon ground turmeric
1 medium onion, roughly chopped
5 cloves garlic
1½ teaspoons chopped fresh ginger
5cm (2 in) cinnamon stick
2 teaspoons salt
1 stem lemon grass *or* 2 strips lemon rind
10 curry leaves
¼ teaspoon fenugreek seeds
1 strip daun pandan *or* rampé leaf, optional
½ cup (4 fl oz) thick coconut milk
1 tablespoon oil *or* melted ghee
1 small onion, finely sliced
2 tablespoons lemon juice

Cut the pork into 5 cm (2 in) pieces and put into a saucepan. Remove stalks and seeds from dried chillies and soak them in half the hot water for 10 minutes. Soak and dissolve tamarind pulp in remaining hot water, strain out seeds and fibres. Put chillies and soaking water into container of electric blender with the turmeric, roughly chopped onion, garlic and ginger and blend until smooth. Pour over pork in pan, add cinnamon and strained tamarind water. Add salt, half each of the lemon grass, curry leaves, fenugreek seeds and pandan or rampé leaf. Bring to the boil, then turn heat low, cover and simmer until pork is tender. Add coconut milk and simmer, uncovered, for 10 minutes longer.

In another pan heat the oil or ghee and fry the sliced onion and the remaining lemon grass, curry leaves, fenugreek seeds and pandan or rampé. When onion is golden brown, turn in the cooked pork mixture and add the lemon juice, stir and simmer on very low heat for about 5 minutes. Serve with rice and accompaniments.

INDONESIA
DRY-FRIED KIDNEY CURRY

Serves: 6

750 g (1½ lb) ox kidney
1 teaspoon finely grated fresh ginger
1 teaspoon finely chopped garlic
1 teaspoon salt
3 tablespoons peanut oil
2 onions, finely chopped *or* sliced
1 teaspoon ground turmeric
2 teaspoons ground coriander
1 teaspoon ground cummin
½ teaspoon ground fennel
½ teaspoon ground black pepper
1 teaspoon chilli powder *or* 2 fresh red
   chillies, seeded and chopped
3 candle nuts, finely grated
2 cups (16 fl oz) coconut milk
1 small stick cinnamon
2 tablespoons tamarind liquid
2 teaspoons sugar

Wash kidneys, remove and discard core. Cut kidneys into small dice. Rub with ginger and garlic crushed with salt and set aside.

Heat oil and fry onions until they are soft and start to colour, stirring frequently. Add turmeric, coriander, cummin, fennel and pepper and stir-fry for 1 minute. Add chillies, candle nuts and kidneys, continue to fry, stirring constantly, until kidneys change colour. Add coconut milk and cinnamon and simmer gently, uncovered, until gravy is thick and reduced. This will take almost 2 hours of gentle simmering. Stir occasionally during simmering period. As mixture thickens it will be necessary to stir more frequently.

Add tamarind liquid and sugar, stir and cook for a few minutes longer. Serve hot.

MALAYSIA
LIVER CURRY

Serves: 4-6

1 kg (2 lb) calves' liver, diced
2 tablespoons desiccated coconut
2 teaspoons chopped garlic
4 candle nuts *or*
   3 Brazil kernels, chopped
4 fresh red chillies
2 teaspoons ground coriander
1 teaspoon ground cummin
1 teaspoon ground fennel
1 stem lemon grass chopped *or*
   2 strips lemon rind
2 teaspoons dried shrimp paste
1½ teaspoons salt
4 tablespoons peanut oil
1 large onion, thinly sliced
½ cup (4 fl oz) coconut milk

Roast desiccated coconut in a dry pan until golden brown. Remove to a plate and when cool put into blender container with the garlic, nuts, chillies, coriander, cummin, fennel, lemon grass, shrimp paste and salt. Blend to a smooth paste adding a little hot water to facilitate blending.

Heat oil in a saucepan and fry onion till soft and golden. Add blended spices and fry till they smell aromatic and oil comes to the surface. Add diced liver and coconut milk and simmer till cooked, stirring contents occasionally. Serve with rice and accompaniments.

SRI LANKA
LIVER CURRY

Even people who don't like eating liver find it most palatable when prepared this way. **Charmaine.**

Serves: 4

500 g (1 lb) calves' liver, sliced
10 black peppercorns
1 teaspoon salt
1 tablespoon ghee *or* oil
1 medium onion, finely chopped
1½ teaspoons finely chopped garlic
1 teaspoon finely chopped fresh ginger
1 stem lemon grass *or* 2 strips lemon rind
¼ teaspoon ground cloves
½ teaspoon ground black pepper
½ teaspoon ground cinnamon
8 curry leaves
3 tablespoons vinegar
2 cups (16 fl oz) coconut milk
2 tablespoons chopped fresh dill *or*
   ½ teaspoon dried dill weed

Wash liver, put into small saucepan with water to cover, add peppercorns and salt and cook until liver is firm, about 15 minutes. Cool.

Cut liver into very small dice. Heat ghee or oil and fry onion, garlic and ginger until soft. Add all ingredients, including liver, and cook uncovered over a low heat until gravy is thick.

SRI LANKA
TRIPE CURRY

A great many ingredients. True. But the end product is worth the effort. **Reuben.**

Serves: 6

1 kg (2 lb) tripe
8 large dried chillies
½ cup (4 fl oz) hot water
2 teaspoons ground cummin
½ teaspoon ground turmeric
½ teaspoon fenugreek seeds
½ teaspoon aromatic ginger (kencur)
8 curry leaves
1 stem lemon grass *or* 2 strips lemon rind
1 strip dried daun pandan *or* rampé
8 whole cardamom pods
4 whole cloves
1 small stick cinnamon
2 medium onions, finely chopped
2 teaspoons finely chopped garlic
1½ teaspoons finely grated fresh ginger
2 cups (16 fl oz) thin coconut milk
1½ teaspoons salt
1 cup (8 fl oz) thick coconut milk
2 tablespoons lemon juice

Wash tripe well and cut into 5 cm (2 in) squares. After removing stalks and seeds, soak chillies in the hot water for 10 minutes, then blend in electric blender until pulverised. Alternatively, use 2 teaspoons chilli powder.

Put tripe and all other ingredients except thick coconut milk and lemon juice, into a large saucepan and bring to the boil. Cover and simmer for 1½ hours or until tripe is tender and gravy smooth and thickened. Add thick coconut milk and simmer, uncovered, stirring for 10 minutes. Remove from heat, add lemon juice and serve with rice.

fish and seafood

An abundance of seafood in coastal areas keeps many millions of Asian people supplied with protein. They eat the fish fresh and they also salt it and dry it in the sun or pickle it in brine. In very poor areas, the diet is literally rice and fish. In dried and salted form fish is p of every meal, sometimes simply fried in a little coconut oil and nibbled at to make the pla rice more interesting.

Even in more affluent circles, salt fish is prepared as an accompaniment. This is cooked with fried onions and dried chillies in a fiery but irresistible sambal.

Fresh fish, prawns, crabs and other sea creatures are more to western taste, however, a they may be curried in as many ways as there are imaginative cooks. Mild coconut milk curries with gentle spices, or hot curries with lots of chilli, or piquant curries with tamarind or vinegar — all have their advocates.

Delicate fish are best cooked in mild curries, but for strongly flavoured fish, try the hot and sour curries.

While small fish such as sprats and sardines are cooked whole, larger fish are cut into serving pieces. Fillets are no problem to divide into portions, but when it comes to fish steaks there is a special way they are cut for curry: small or medium steaks may simply be halved crossways, but larger fish steaks are cut into four, six or eight as illustrated below.

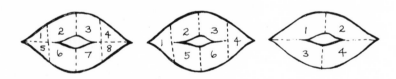

SRI LANKA
FISH CURRY WITH TOMATO

There are many types of fish curry in Sri Lanka — some mild, some hot, some very acid, some mildly piquant. This comes in the final category. **Charmaine.**

Serves: 4-5

500 g (1 lb) fish steaks (kingfish, tuna,
   Spanish mackerel, mullet)
1 teaspoon ground turmeric
1 teaspoon salt
oil for frying
1 large onion, roughly chopped
3 cloves garlic
2 teaspoons finely chopped fresh ginger
1 medium-size ripe tomato, chopped
2 tablespoons oil
1 tablespoon Ceylon curry powder (see page 17)
1 teaspoon chilli powder
salt to taste
2 cups (16 fl oz) coconut milk

Wash and dry fish well and rub all over with turmeric and salt. Cut each steak into serving pieces. Heat oil in a frying pan and fry the fish until golden brown on both sides. Drain.

Put onion, garlic, ginger and tomato in container of electric blender and blend to a smooth paste. Heat oil in a saucepan and fry the blended ingredients for a few minutes, until oil begins to separate from mixture. Add the curry and chilli powders and about a teaspoon of salt, then the coconut milk, and bring to the boil, stirring. Simmer for a few minutes, then add the fish and simmer for 10 minutes. Serve with rice and accompaniments.

INDIA
FISH CURRY

(Picture on opposite page)

Serves: 4

500 g (1 lb) fish steaks *or* fillets
   or small whole fish
2 tablespoons oil
6-8 curry leaves
1 medium onion, finely sliced
1 teaspoon finely chopped garlic
1 tablespoon finely grated fresh ginger
1 tablespoon ground coriander
2 teaspoons ground cummin
½ teaspoon ground turmeric
½-1 teaspoon chilli powder
½ teaspoon ground fenugreek
2 cups (16 fl oz) coconut milk
1½ teaspoons salt *or* to taste
lemon juice to taste

Wash fish well. If small fish are used, clean and scale them. If large steaks or fillets are used, cut them into serving pieces. Heat oil and fry the curry leaves until slightly brown, then add onion, garlic and ginger and fry until onion is soft and golden. Add all the ground spices and fry, stirring, until they smell aromatic. Add coconut milk and salt and bring to the boil, stirring.

Simmer uncovered for 10 minutes, then put in the fish, ladle the liquid over it and simmer until fish is cooked, approximately 10-15 minutes. Remove from heat and stir in lemon juice to taste.

Fish Curry, recipe on opposite page

Burmese lacquer ware holds Fish Ball Curry, recipe on opposite page; Chicken Curry with Noodles, recipe page 79; and Dry Balachaung, a favourite Burmese accompaniment, recipe page 108.

BURMA
FISH BALL CURRY

(Picture on opposite page)

Our favourite fish curry, full of flavour and well worth the extra trouble of making the fish balls. This recipe was taught me by my grandmother, Alice Gray, who was born and lived most of her life in Burma.
Charmaine.

Serves: 6

Fish Balls:
1 kg (2 lb) jewfish *or* cod fillets
2½ teaspoons salt
½ teaspoon pepper
1 medium onion, finely chopped
½ teaspoon finely chopped garlic
1½ teaspoons finely grated fresh ginger
2 tablespoons lemon juice, strained
1 tablespoon finely chopped fresh
    coriander leaves *or* dill
2 slices white bread, soaked in hot water and
    squeezed dry
1 tablespoon fish sauce *or*
    1 teaspoon anchovy paste *or* sauce, optional

Curry:
¼ cup (2 fl oz) light sesame oil or corn oil
3 medium onions, finely chopped
3 teaspoons finely chopped garlic
1 tablespoon finely chopped fresh ginger
1 teaspoon ground turmeric
1-2 teaspoons chilli powder, optional
1 teaspoon paprika, optional
2 tomatoes, peeled and chopped
1½ teaspoons salt
1 teaspoon dried shrimp paste
1½ cups (12 fl oz) hot water
2 tablespoons chopped fresh coriander leaves
2 tablespoons lemon juice

Fish Balls: With a sharp knife remove skin from fish. Finely mince fish, taking care to remove bones. (To do this without a mincer, cut fillets in thin slices lengthways, then chop finely across.) Put minced fish in a large bowl, add remaining ingredients. Mix thoroughly with the hands. Shape the mixture into walnut-size balls (this quantity should make 24 balls).

Curry: Heat oil in large saucepan and fry onion, garlic and ginger until soft and golden. Add turmeric, remove from heat and add chilli powder and paprika (if used), tomato and salt. (In Burmese cooking the amount of chilli used would be enough to give a red colour to the gravy, but the paprika is suggested here as a substitute for a portion of it, with chilli used to suit individual tastes.)

Wrap dried shrimp paste in aluminium foil and cook under hot griller for a few minutes on each side. Unwrap, dissolve in hot water and add to the gravy. Cook gravy until tomato is soft and pulpy. If gravy seems too reduced, add a little hot water. There should be enough gravy to almost cover the fish balls.

Gently put the fish balls in the gravy and simmer over a moderate heat until they are cooked, about 20 minutes. Shake pan gently from time to time. Do not stir until fish is cooked and firm, or the balls might break. Stir in the chopped coriander leaves and lemon juice and cook 5 minutes longer. Serve with white rice and balachaung (see page 108).

INDONESIA
SQUID CURRY

Serves: 4

500 g (1 lb) fresh squid
1 medium onion, finely chopped
1 teaspoon finely chopped garlic
1 teaspoon finely grated fresh ginger
1 teaspoon salt
1 teaspoon chilli powder
½ teaspoon dried shrimp paste
1¾ cups (14 fl oz) coconut milk
4 candle nuts *or* Brazil nuts, grated
1 stem lemon grass, finely sliced *or*
 1 teaspoon grated lemon rind
1 teaspoon sugar
4 tablespoons tamarind liquid *or*
 lemon juice to taste

Clean squid, removing head and ink sac. Wash well
inside and out and rub away spotted skin from body.
Cut each squid in halves lengthways, then into bite-
size pieces. Put all other ingredients except sugar and
tamarind or lemon into a saucepan and bring to simmering point, stirring. Allow to simmer, uncovered,
until thickened. Stir occasionally.

 Add squid, simmer for 5 to 6 minutes. Add sugar and
tamarind or lemon juice, taste and add more salt if
necessary. Serve hot with rice and vegetables.

THAILAND
GREEN CURRY OF FISH

(Picture page 1)

*The predominance of fresh herbs gives this curry a
greenish colour and a good flavour.* **Charmaine**

Serves: 4

500 g (1 lb) fish steaks
2½ cups (20 fl oz) coconut milk
2 tablespoons green curry paste (see page 15)
2 sprigs citrus leaves
1 teaspoon salt
1 tablespoon fish sauce
1 *or* 2 green chillies, seeded and chopped
2 tablespoons finely chopped fresh basil

Wash fish well and trim any spines with kitchen scis-
sors. Bring coconut milk to the boil with the curry
paste, stirring constantly. Add fish, reduce heat and
simmer with citrus leaves, salt and fish sauce until the
fish is cooked through, about 15 minutes.

 Add chillies and fresh basil and simmer a few minutes longer, then serve with white rice.

INDIA

FISH CURRY WITH FENUGREEK LEAVES

Serves: 4

500 g (1 lb) fish fillets
1 large onion, finely sliced
2 tablespoons peanut oil
1 teaspoon finely chopped garlic
1 teaspoon finely chopped fresh ginger
2 teaspoons curry leaves
1 tablespoon dried fenugreek leaves
1 teaspoon ground turmeric
1 teaspoon chilli powder
½ teaspoon ground cardamom
½ teaspoon ground cinnamon
pinch of ground cloves
rind of ½ lemon
¼ cup (2 fl oz) thick coconut milk
1½ (12 fl oz) cups warm water
salt to taste

Heat oil and fry sliced onion till golden brown. Lower heat, add garlic, ginger, curry leaves, fenugreek leaves, turmeric, chilli powder, cardamom, cinnamon, cloves and lemon rind. Stir for 2 minutes then add coconut milk with the warm water. Add salt, stir and simmer for 10 minutes. Add fish fillets, ensuring fish is coated with the sauce, and simmer until fish is cooked. Serve with rice or Indian bread.

INDIA

FISH WHITE CURRY

For children, leave out the green chillies — the coconut milk gravy gives flavour to plain steamed rice. **Charmaine.**

Serves: 4-6

750 g (1½ lb) fish fillets *or* steaks
lemon juice
1 teaspoon ground turmeric
1½ teaspoons salt
2 tablespoons oil *or* ghee
2 small onions, finely sliced
2 teaspoons finely sliced garlic
3 slices fresh ginger, cut into slivers
8-10 curry leaves
3 fresh green chillies, seeded and cut in half
 lengthways
2 cups (16 fl oz) thin coconut milk
1 cup (8 fl oz) thick coconut milk
lime *or* lemon juice to taste
salt to taste

Wash the fish and rub over with lemon juice, turmeric and salt.

Heat the oil in a saucepan and on low heat fry the onions, garlic, ginger, curry leaves and chillies until onions are soft. Stir frequently and do not allow any of the ingredients to brown. Add the thin coconut milk and stir while it comes to simmering point. Add the fish and cook slowly, uncovered, for 10 minutes.

Add thick coconut milk, stir gently, heat through and remove from heat, then add lime or lemon juice and salt to taste. Serve with white rice and a coconut chutney.

FISH KORMA

A very rich dish, typical of North India. **Reuben.**

Serves: 4-6

750 g (1½ lb) fish fillets
lemon juice
1 teaspoon salt
1 teaspoon ground black pepper
1 teaspoon ground turmeric
oil for frying
1 large onion, finely sliced
1 medium onion, roughly chopped
1 teaspoon chopped garlic
1 tablespoon chopped fresh ginger
2 *or* 3 fresh red chillies, seeded
2 tablespoons blanched almonds
1 tablespoon white poppy seeds, optional
2 teaspoons ground cummin
2 teaspoons ground coriander
¼ teaspoon ground cardamom
¼ teaspoon ground cinnamon
small pinch ground cloves
¼ teaspoon saffron strands
2 tablespoons boiling water
½ cup (4 fl oz) natural yoghurt
salt to taste
2 tablespoons chopped fresh coriander

Wash and dry fish, cut into large serving pieces and rub with lemon juice, salt, pepper and turmeric. Heat oil in a frying pan for shallow frying and on high heat brown the fish quickly on both sides. Lift out on to a plate. In the same oil fry the sliced onion until golden brown, remove and set aside.

Put chopped onion, garlic, ginger, chillies, almonds, poppy seeds into blender jar and purée. If necessary add a little water. Add ground spices and blend once more, briefly.

Pour off all but about 2 tablespoons oil from pan and fry the blended mixture until colour changes and it gives out a pleasing aroma. The mixture should be stirred constantly while frying and care taken that it does not stick to pan and burn. Add ¼ cup water to blender container and swirl out any remaining spice mixture. Add to pan.

Pound saffron strands in mortar and pestle, add boiling water and stir, add to mixture in pan. Add yoghurt, stir and simmer gently for a few minutes, then add fish pieces, turning them carefully in the sauce. Add salt to taste. Cover and simmer for about 10 minutes, then sprinkle with fresh coriander and serve hot with rice.

FISH IN COCONUT MILK & SPICES

Serves: 6

750 g (1½ lb) firm dark fish steaks (tuna, mackerel, kingfish)
salt to taste
juice of half a lemon
2 onions, finely chopped
1½ teaspoons finely chopped garlic
2 teaspoons finely grated fresh ginger
1 teaspoon ground turmeric
½ teaspoon dried shrimp paste
1 teaspoon sambal ulek *or* chilli powder
1 stem lemon grass *or* 2 strips lemon rind
1 teaspoon salt
1½ cups (12 fl oz) thin coconut milk
2 tablespoons chopped fresh basil
¼ cup (2 fl oz) tamarind liquid
1 cup (8 fl oz) thick coconut milk

Wash fish, rub with a little salt and lemon juice and set aside. Combine onions, garlic, ginger, turmeric, shrimp paste, sambal ulek, lemon grass and salt in a saucepan with thin coconut milk. Bring to simmering point and simmer uncovered until onions are soft and liquid thickened.

Add fish, basil and tamarind liquid and simmer until fish is cooked. Stir in the thick coconut milk and heat through but do not boil, stirring so that coconut milk does not curdle. Serve with white rice, vegetables and sambals.

SRI LANKA
FISH CURRY WITH TAMARIND

Serves: 4

500 g (1 lb) firm fish steaks *or* fillets
1 rounded tablespoon tamarind pulp
½ cup (4 fl oz) hot water
1½ tablespoons Ceylon curry powder (see page 17)
1 teaspoon salt
¼ teaspoon ground turmeric
1 teaspoon chilli powder
3 tablespoons oil
6 curry leaves
¼ teaspoon fenugreek seeds
1 medium onion, finely chopped
1 teaspoon finely chopped garlic

Wash and dry fish and cut into serving pieces. Soak tamarind pulp in hot water, allow to cool, squeeze to dissolve pulp. Strain through fine nylon sieve and discard seeds and fibres. Combine tamarind liquid with curry powder, salt, turmeric, chilli powder and marinate fish for 20 minutes.

Heat oil and fry the curry leaves and fenugreek seeds until golden brown, then add onion and garlic and continue to fry on medium heat until onion is golden, stirring occasionally. Add fish and marinade, cover and cook over low heat for 10 minutes. Uncover and cook for a further 10 minutes. Serve with white rice and vegetable curries.

MALAYSIA
FISH CURRY

Serves: 4

500 g (1 lb) firm fish steaks
2 medium onions, roughly chopped
2 cloves garlic
2 teaspoons chopped fresh ginger
1 teaspoon sambal ulek *or* chilli powder
1 cup (8 fl oz) thin coconut milk
1 tablespoon ground coriander
1 teaspoon ground cummin
½ teaspoon ground fennel
½ teaspoon ground turmeric
1 stem fresh lemon grass *or*
   2 strips thinly peeled lemon rind
6 curry leaves
2 tablespoons lemon juice
1 teaspoon salt
½ cup (4 fl oz) thick coconut milk

Cut fish steaks into serving pieces. Put onions, garlic, ginger and sambal ulek into blender container and blend to a smooth paste, adding a tablespoon of thin coconut milk if necessary. Scrape the blended mixture into a saucepan, wash out blender with the thin coconut milk and add to saucepan together with the ground spices, lemon rind and curry leaves.

Bring to the boil, reduce heat and simmer for about 8 minutes, then add the fish, tamarind liquid and salt and simmer for 5 minutes. Add thick coconut milk and stir gently until curry reaches simmering point once more. Serve with rice.

HOT FISH CURRY WITH SHRIMP PASTE

Serves: 4

500 g (1 lb) fish fillets
2 tablespoons oil
1 large onion, sliced
1 teaspoon dried shrimp paste
1 teaspoon finely chopped garlic
2 tablespoons ground roasted peanuts
 or crunchy peanut butter
1 teaspoon ground cummin
4 green chillies, chopped
 or 2 teaspoons chilli powder
1 teaspoon turmeric
1 teaspoon laos powder
½ cup (4 fl oz) hot water
¼ cup (2 fl oz) thick coconut milk
salt to taste

Heat oil in a saucepan and brown sliced onion on medium heat. Add shrimp paste and garlic, lower heat and stir for a few minutes. Add ground peanuts, cummin, chilli, turmeric and laos and cook 1 minute longer.

Add water, then stir, cover and simmer till mixture smells cooked and the oil comes to the top. Add coconut milk and salt, stir and add fish fillets. Cover and simmer about 10 minutes and serve with steamed rice.

FISH CURRY WITH COCONUT

Some of the finest dishes we ever had were at the beach resorts in Goa, Madras, Mahabalipuram and Bombay. **Reuben.**
In South India they would use coconut oil instead of ghee; and in Bengal mustard oil provides the flavour typical of the cooking of that area. But for those who are not used to these distinctive oils, ghee (clarified butter) or a light, neutral oil (not olive oil) is more acceptable. **Charmaine.**

Serves: 6

750 g (1½ lb) fish steaks
lemon juice, salt and pepper
6 large dried red chillies
2 tablespoons desiccated coconut
1 tablespoon coriander seeds
2 teaspoons cummin seeds
¼ teaspoon fenugreek seeds
4 teaspoons finely chopped garlic
1 teaspoon finely chopped fresh ginger
1 tablespoon tamarind pulp *or*
 1 teaspoon instant tamarind
½ cup (4 fl oz) hot water
2 tablespoons ghee *or* oil
1 large onion, finely chopped
1½ cups (12 fl oz) coconut milk
1½ teaspoons salt

Wash fish, rub over with lemon juice, salt and pepper and set aside. Soak the chillies in hot water for 10 minutes.

In a dry pan roast the coconut, stirring constantly, until brown. Remove coconut to a plate and dry roast the coriander, cummin and fenugreek seeds, shaking pan or stirring, until brown. Put the chillies, coconut, spices, garlic and ginger into container of electric blender and blend to a smooth paste, adding a little water if necessary. Soak tamarind pulp in hot water, squeeze to dissolve, strain. Or dissolve instant tamarind in hot water. Reserve tamarind liquid.

Heat ghee in a heavy saucepan and fry the chopped onion until soft. Add the ground mixture and fry on medium heat, stirring, until it darkens in colour and smells cooked. Add the coconut milk, salt, tamarind liquid and bring slowly to simmering point, stirring to prevent curdling. Add the fish and simmer for 10 minutes or until fish is cooked. Do not cover. Serve hot with rice.

Note: Ground coriander, cummin and fenugreek may be used instead of whole seeds, but roast them on a low heat, stirring constantly and taking care that they do not burn.

INDONESIA
BALINESE STYLE FISH

Serves: 6

1 kg (2 lb) fish steaks
2 tablespoons peanut oil
2 medium onions, finely chopped
1 teaspoon finely chopped garlic
1½ teaspoons finely grated fresh ginger
1½ teaspoons sambal ulek (see Glossary) *or* fresh
    chilli paste
1 teaspoon finely grated lemon rind
1 teaspoon laos powder
2 tablespoons lemon juice
2 tablespoons palm sugar *or* substitute
2 tablespoons dark soy sauce
½ teaspoon salt
peanut oil for frying

Wash fish, dry on absorbent paper towels and cut into serving portions. Heat about 2 tablespoons oil in a small saucepan and fry the onions until soft. Add garlic and ginger and stir over medium heat until golden brown. Add sambal ulek, lemon rind, laos, lemon juice, sugar, soy sauce and salt and simmer for 2 or 3 minutes. Set aside.

Heat peanut oil for deep frying and fry the fish until golden brown on both sides. Drain, put on serving plate and spoon the sauce over. Serve with rice.

SRI LANKA
FRIED SQUID CURRY

Serves: 4-6

about 1 kg (2 lb) squid
2 medium onions, finely sliced
2 teaspoons finely chopped garlic
2 teaspoons finely grated fresh ginger
1 teaspoon ground turmeric
1 teaspoon chilli powder, optional
2 tablespoons Ceylon curry powder (see page 17)
½ teaspoon whole fenugreek seeds
1 cinnamon stick
1 stem fresh lemon grass *or* 2 strips lemon rind
10 curry leaves
3 tablespoons vinegar
3 cups (24 fl oz) coconut milk
1½ teaspoons ghee *or* oil for frying

Clean squid, removing ink sac and discarding head. Cut into rings. Put in a deep saucepan with all the ingredients except ghee. Bring to the boil, then simmer for about 1 hour or until squid is tender and the gravy reduced to a small quantity.

Drain pieces of squid from the gravy and, in another pan, heat the ghee and fry the squid. Pour the gravy into the pan in which the squid are fried, simmer for a minute or two longer and serve with white rice and sambols.

INDIA
MADRAS PRAWN CURRY

Serves: 6

1 kg (2 lb) raw prawns
1 tablespoon desiccated coconut
1 tablespoon ground rice
2 cups (16 fl oz) coconut milk
2 tablespoons ghee *or* oil
12 curry leaves
2 medium onions, finely chopped
2½ teaspoons finely chopped garlic
3 teaspoons finely grated fresh ginger
2 tablespoons Madras curry powder (see page 16) *or*
    Madras curry paste (see page 15)
1 teaspoon chilli powder, optional
2 teaspoons paprika
1½ teaspoons salt
2 tablespoons lemon juice

Shell and de-vein prawns. Put desiccated coconut into a dry pan and toast over medium heat, shaking pan or stirring constantly until coconut is golden brown. Remove from pan and do the same with the ground rice. Put both into blender container with about half a cup (4 fl oz) of the coconut milk and blend until smooth and coconut is very finely ground.

Heat ghee in a saucepan and fry the curry leaves for 1 minute. Add onions, garlic and ginger and fry until golden brown, stirring with a wooden spoon. Add curry powder, chilli powder and paprika and fry on low heat, stirring. Do not let the spices burn. Add blended mixture, rest of coconut milk and salt, stir while bringing to simmering point. Do not cover. Simmer gently for 15 minutes, stirring occasionally.

Add prawns, stir to mix, simmer for further 10-15 minutes or until prawns are cooked and gravy thick. Stir in lemon juice. Serve with rice.

BURMA
PRAWN CURRY WITH GRAVY

One of my favourite ways of cooking prawns. The addition of green herbs at the end of cooking gives extra flavour. **Charmaine.**

Serves: 4

500 g (1 lb) shelled prawns
1 large onion
3 cloves garlic
1 teaspoon finely grated fresh ginger
½ teaspoon ground turmeric
½ teaspoon chilli powder
3 tablespoons light sesame oil *or* corn oil
pinch each of ground cloves, ground cardamom
    and ground fennel
1 large potato, diced
2 ripe tomatoes, chopped
½ cup (4 fl oz) thin coconut milk
½ cup (4 fl oz) thick coconut milk
1 tablespoon chopped coriander leaves
2 tablespoons chopped spring onion leaves
salt to taste

De-vein prawns, prepare and cook basic ingredients as described on page 21. Add ground cloves, cardamom, fennel, potato and tomato and stir well. Cook for 10 minutes with lid on pan. Add thin coconut milk and gently simmer uncovered for 10 minutes. Then add prawns and thick coconut milk and simmer, stirring frequently, until prawns are cooked, about 5 minutes.

Add coriander leaves and cook a further 2 or 3 minutes, then remove from heat and stir in the spring onion. Taste and add more salt if required. Serve hot with white rice and accompaniments.

SRI LANKA
SALT FISH & EGGPLANT CURRY

You may think this is a strange combination, but believe me, it is so tasty that whenever I visit my old home in Sri Lanka I request this favourite curry. **Charmaine.**

Serves: 6

250 g (8 oz) dried salted fish
2 medium eggplants, about 500 g (1 lb)
1 teaspoon ground turmeric
1 teaspoon salt
12 large fresh sweet chillies
oil for frying
10 cloves garlic, peeled and left whole
1 large onion, finely sliced
3 cups (24 fl oz) coconut milk
3 tablespoons Ceylon curry powder (see page 17)
small stick cinnamon
walnut size piece of tamarind pulp
¼ cup (2 fl oz) malt vinegar
½ teaspoon salt, *or* to taste
1-2 teaspoons sugar

Wash the dried fish, drain, then cut into 5 cm (2 in) pieces. Slice the eggplants thickly, rub each slice with turmeric and salt and set aside for 30 minutes. Wash chillies, slit and remove seeds. Drain liquid that has come from eggplant slices and dry each slice on kitchen paper.

Heat about quarter cup (2 fl oz) oil in a frying pan and fry separately the dried fish, eggplant, chillies, garlic, and onion removing each to a dish as fried. It may be necessary to replenish the oil as it is used up, for the eggplant absorbs quite a lot.

Put the coconut milk into a saucepan with the curry powder and cinnamon, tamarind dissolved in vinegar, and salt. Stir until it comes to the boil, add fried ingredients and keep stirring frequently as the mixture cooks, uncovered. When it is thick, add sugar and stir to dissolve before serving.

Note: Sweet chillies are slightly wider in shape and milder in flavour than hot chillies. They are the variety popular with Indian and Yugoslavian cooks.

KAMPUCHEA
PRAWN & SWEET GOURD CURRY

Serves: 6

500 g (1 lb) large raw prawns
1 sweet gourd *or* tender marrow *or*
  2 green cucumbers
5 cloves garlic
1 small onion, roughly chopped
2 teaspoons finely chopped fresh ginger
½ teaspoon chilli powder
½ teaspoon ground fennel
2 teaspoons ground coriander
¼ teaspoon ground turmeric
4 tablespoons oil
2 cups (16 fl oz) coconut milk
1 stem lemon grass, bruised
2 tablespoons lemon juice
1 teaspoon sugar, optional
1 tablespoon fish sauce

Shell and de-vein prawns. Peel gourd or cucumbers, cut in halves lengthways, scoop out seeds and cut in thick slices. Put garlic, onion and ginger into container of electric blender and blend to a purée. Mix in the ground spices.

Heat oil in a pan and fry the blended ingredients until they are well cooked and the oil starts to show around the edges, much as described in the basic method for Burmese curries (see page 21.) Add the prawns and stir fry for 3 minutes, then add coconut milk and bring to simmering point. Add sliced gourd or cucumber, remaining seasonings, and stir gently until vegetables are cooked and tender but not too soft. Serve with rice.

INDIA
PRAWN COCONUT MILK CURRY

Serves: 4

750 g (1½ lb) large raw prawns
1 tablespoon ghee *or* oil
2 medium onions, thinly sliced
1 teaspoon finely chopped garlic
1 teaspoon finely grated fresh ginger
2 fresh red *or* green chillies, slit and seeded
1 teaspoon ground turmeric
8 curry leaves
2 cups (16 fl oz) coconut milk
1 teaspoon salt
lemon juice to taste

Wash prawns well. Shell and de-vein if liked, but Indian cooks say the prawns should be in their shells, for they retain more flavour this way. Heat ghee and fry the onions, garlic and ginger until onions are soft but do not let them brown. Add chillies, turmeric and curry leaves and fry 1 minute longer. Add coconut milk and salt and stir while bringing to simmering point.

Simmer uncovered for 10 minutes, then add prawns and cook for 10 minutes. Remove from heat and add lemon juice to taste.

BURMA
PRAWN CURRY, DRY

A very easy curry, but one of the most delicious. Don't neglect the fresh herbs added last of all. **Reuben.**

Serves: 4

500 g (1 lb) shelled prawns
1 large onion
3-4 cloves garlic
1 teaspoon finely grated fresh ginger
½ teaspoon ground turmeric
¼ teaspoon chilli powder
3 tablespoons light sesame oil *or* corn oil
1 tablespoon chopped fresh coriander leaves
1 teaspoon salt *or* to taste
2 tablespoons chopped spring onion leaves

De-vein prawns, rinse and drain. Prepare and cook basic ingredients as on page 21. When well cooked and sizzling, put in the prawns and stir well. Sprinkle with the fresh coriander leaves, cover and cook 3 or 4 minutes or until prawns are done. Turn off heat, stir in the spring onion and serve hot with white rice and accompaniments.

MALAYSIA
DRIED PRAWN CURRY

Serves: 3-4

250 g (8 oz) dried prawns
1 large onion, roughly chopped
2 teaspoons chopped garlic
8 dried red chillies, soaked
5 candle nuts
    or Brazil nuts, roughly chopped
2 teaspoons dried shrimp paste
1 teaspoon laos powder
3 tablespoons oil
1 stem lemon grass, finely chopped *or*
    rind of half lemon
¼ cup (2 oz) tamarind liquid
1 teaspoon salt
¾ cup (6 fl oz) thick coconut milk

Soak prawns in hot water for 1 hour, drain and set aside. Place onion, garlic, dried chillies, nuts, dried shrimp paste and laos powder in blender container and blend to a smooth paste, adding a little hot water to facilitate blending.

Heat saucepan, add oil and when hot add lemon grass. Stir in the blended spices and cook until it smells fragrant and oil comes to the surface. Add the drained prawns and cook further 10 minutes on low heat, stirring occasionally. Add tamarind liquid and salt and cook for a further 5 minutes. Stir in coconut milk and serve with rice.

PRAWN CURRY

Serves: 4

500 g (1 lb) raw prawns
4-6 dry red chillies
½ teaspoon cummin seeds
¼ teaspoon ground black pepper
1½ teaspoons chopped garlic
1 teaspoon finely chopped fresh ginger
1 teaspoon ground turmeric
3 tablespoons oil
2 medium onions, chopped
1 ripe tomato, chopped
1 teaspoon salt
2 tablespoons vinegar

Shell and de-vein prawns, rinse well and drain in colander. Discard seeds and stalks of chillies, and soak chillies in hot water for 5 minutes. Put chillies, cummin, pepper, garlic, ginger and turmeric into electric blender and blend at high speed, adding a little oil to facilitate blending. If blender is not available, substitute 2 teaspoons chilli powder for dry chillies, ground cummin for cummin seeds, and finely grate the garlic and ginger. Mix these ingredients together with the turmeric.

Heat oil and fry onions until soft and golden. Add blended mixture and fry for a few minutes, then add the tomato, salt and vinegar. Cover and cook until tomato is reduced to pulp. Add prawns, stir well, cover and cook until prawns are done, about 10 minutes. Serve with white rice.

RED PRAWN CURRY

(Picture page 37)

Sri Lankan curries are very hot and in this recipe paprika is substituted for part of the chilli to give the right colour without too much heat. **Charmaine.**

Serves: 6

750 g (1½ lb) small raw prawns
1 medium onion, finely chopped
1½ teaspoons finely chopped garlic
1 teaspoon finely grated fresh ginger
small stick cinnamon
¼ teaspoon fenugreek seeds
few curry leaves
small stem lemon grass, bruised,
  or 2 strips lemon rind
1 strip daun pandan or rampé leaf
½ teaspoon ground turmeric
1½ teaspoons chilli powder
2 teaspoons paprika
1 teaspoon salt
2 cups (16 fl oz) coconut milk
good squeeze lemon juice

Wash prawns and remove heads, but leave shells on. (In Sri Lanka prawns are often cooked in their shells, for better flavour.) Put all ingredients, except lemon juice, into a saucepan and bring slowly to simmering point. Simmer uncovered for 20 minutes or until onions are soft. Add lemon juice and stir. Taste and add more salt or lemon if required. Serve with rice, vegetable curries and a sambol.

PRAWN CURRY

(Picture page 128)

Serves: 4

500 g (1 lb) large fresh prawns
1 large onion, roughly chopped
6 dried red chillies
2 fresh red chillies
2 teaspoons chopped garlic
1 teaspoon laos powder
1 teaspoon dried shrimp paste
1 teaspoon ground turmeric
2 tablespoons peanut oil
2 tablespoons lemon juice
1 tablespoon sugar
1 teaspoon salt

Garnish
2 tablespoons chopped coriander leaves

Wash prawns but do not remove heads and shells. Place onion, dried and fresh chillies, garlic, laos, dried shrimp paste and turmeric in blender jar and blend to a paste on high speed, using a little water to facilitate blending.

Heat oil in a saucepan and fry the ground spices until they start to smell fragrant. Stir in the lemon juice, sugar and salt, add the prawns and stir till they turn red. Cover and simmer for 5 minutes, garnish with chopped coriander leaves and serve with rice.

PRAWN RED CURRY

Serves: 4

500 g (1 lb) raw prawns
2 cups (16 fl oz) coconut milk
2 tablespoons red curry paste (see page 18)
1-2 tablespoons fish sauce *or* 1 teaspoon salt
1 fresh red chilli, seeded

Shell and de-vein prawns, but reserve heads. Wash prawn heads well, discarding only the hard top shell. Put the coconut milk into a pan with the curry paste, fish sauce and the fresh chilli. Bring slowly to simmering point, stirring. Add prawns and prawn heads and cook uncovered, stirring frequently, on low heat until prawns are cooked and flavours mellow, about 15 minutes.

This curry is even better prepared ahead and reheated when required. Serve hot with white rice and other accompaniments. The prawn heads have a wonderful flavour and may be served as part of the curry.

PRAWN VINDALOO

Use stainless steel or enamel pans, especially for acid curries like this one. In Asia such dishes are cooked in earthenware pots. **Charmaine.**

Serves: 4

500 g (1 lb) large raw prawns
2 medium onions, roughly chopped
2 teaspoons chopped garlic
2 fresh red *or* green chillies, chopped
2 teaspoons chopped fresh ginger
¼ cup (2 fl oz) white vinegar
1½ teaspoons ground cummin
1 teaspoon garam masala
1 teaspoon ground turmeric
1 teaspoon salt
4 tablespoons oil
1 large onion, finely sliced
3 tablespoons lemon juice

Shell and de-vein prawns, wash and drain well. Rub half the turmeric and salt over the prawns. Put chopped onion, garlic, chillies, ginger and vinegar in electric blender and grind to a pulp. If blender is not available crush the garlic, grate ginger finely and chop onions very fine. Add ground cummin and garam masala, remaining turmeric and salt.

Heat oil in a saucepan and fry the sliced onion until soft and turning brown. Add the blended mixture and fry, stirring, until it is well cooked and oil separates from the mass. Add the prawns, bring to a slow simmer and cook for 8-10 minutes. Stir in lemon juice and serve with rice.

SRI LANKA
CRAB CURRY

(Picture page 127)

A very special dish that is usually served only with plain white rice, nothing else to distract from the superb flavour of the crab and the spicy sauce. **Charmaine.**

Serves: 4-6

2 large crabs
3 medium onions, roughly chopped
6 cloves garlic
2 teaspoons finely grated fresh ginger
½ teaspoon fenugreek seeds
10 curry leaves
8 cm (3 in) stick cinnamon
1-2 teaspoons chilli powder
1 teaspoon ground turmeric
3 teaspoons salt
4 cups (32 fl oz) thin coconut milk
2 tablespoons desiccated coconut
1 tablespoon ground rice
2 cups (16 fl oz) thick coconut milk
3 tablespoons lemon juice

Remove large shells of crabs and discard fibrous tissue found under the shell. Divide each crab into 4 portions, breaking each body in half and separating large claws from body. Leave legs attached to body.

Purée onion, garlic and ginger in electric blender. Heat oil in large saucepan and fry this purée, stirring for about 10 minutes. Add fenugreek, curry leaves, cinnamon, chilli powder, turmeric, salt and thin coconut milk. Cover and simmer gently 30 minutes. Add crabs and cook for 20 minutes if using raw crabs. Cook for only 5-7 minutes if cooked crabs are used. If pan is not large enough, simmer half the pieces of crab at a time. Crab should be submerged in sauce while cooking.

Heat desiccated coconut and ground rice separately in a dry frying pan over moderate heat, stirring constantly to prevent burning, until each is golden brown. Put in an electric blender container, add half the thick coconut milk, cover and blend on high speed 1 minute. Add to curry with lemon juice. Wash out blender with remaining coconut milk and add. Simmer uncovered a further 10 minutes. Serve with boiled rice.

INDIA
CRAB CURRY

We tasted this at the Fort Aguada beach resort in Goa. What a beautiful place and what a beautiful meal. **Reuben.**

Serves: 4-6

2 or 3 medium-sized crabs
3 tablespoons oil *or* ghee
2 medium onions, finely chopped
2 teaspoons finely grated garlic
2 teaspoons finely grated fresh ginger
2 fresh red chillies, seeded and sliced
2 teaspoons ground coriander
2 teaspoons ground cummin
2 tablespoons ground almonds *or* white poppy seeds
2 bay leaves (tej pattar)
1½ teaspoons salt *or* to taste
1 cup (8 fl oz) tomato purée
1½ cups (12 fl oz) coconut milk
3 tablespoons chopped fresh coriander

Remove large shells of crabs and discard all fibrous tissue from under the shell. Divide each crab into 4 portions, breaking the body in half and separating the large, meaty claws from the body. Legs should be left attached to the body.

Heat the oil in a large saucepan and fry the onions, garlic, ginger and chillies until onions are soft and golden. Add coriander, cummin and ground almonds and fry for a minute or so longer. Then add the bay leaves, salt, tomato purée and coconut milk and stir while bringing to a gentle simmer.

Put in the crabs and cook, uncovered, for 15-20 minutes or until the crabs are done. If pan is not large enough, cook in two lots. When cooked the shells will turn bright red and the flesh becomes white and opaque. If cooked crabs are used, reduce cooking time by half. Add coriander leaves during last 5 minutes. Serve with plain boiled rice.

poultry

Chickens are the most popular birds in Asian cooking, followed by ducks, snipe, guinea fowl, teal and paddy birds. Turkeys too make an occasional appearance, but goose is rarer than peafowl.

All are delicious when curried and sometimes I have referred to cutting the bird in 'curry pieces'. This means cutting pieces smaller than merely jointing, and enables the flavours to penetrate the meat readily.

To cut a chicken for curry, first joint the bird, then with a heavy cleaver cut each thigh in two. The breast is divided down the centre and each half cut into two. Wings are divided in two pieces, the first joint which looks like a small drumstick is detached from the breast, then the second joint and wing tip are separated from the first joint. Though the bony back the bird is cut into three or four pieces and cooked with the curry for flavour, it is not counted as a serving piece because there is very little meat on the back except for the two 'oysters' of flesh just above the thigh joint. Liver and giblets are also included in the curry, and indeed are so delicious that in the intimacy of family meals, they may be the bone of contention.

If the chicken weight is around 1.5 kg (3 lb), use the method described above. But if it is much smaller, the breast should only be divided into halves. On the other hand if it is much larger, even the drumsticks should be chopped in two.

Chicken is so versatile, it is equally delicious in gently spiced coconut milk curries, rich North Indian dishes and hot Sri Lankan, Malaysian or South Indian curries, not to mention the numerous Indonesian dishes.

But when cooking duck, which is stronger in flavour and has richer meat, it is the hot, sour, vindaloo type of curry that suits it to perfection.

INDONESIA
CHICKEN IN COCONUT MILK

A wonderfully fragrant preparation, spicy but not hot. A fine introduction to curries. **Charmaine.**

Serves: 4-6

1.5 kg (3 lb) roasting chicken *or* chicken pieces
1½ teaspoons finely grated garlic
1 teaspoon salt
½ teaspoon ground black pepper
1½ teaspoons finely grated fresh ginger
3 candle nuts *or* Brazil nuts, finely grated
3 teaspoons ground coriander
1 teaspoon ground cummin
½ teaspoon ground fennel
½ teaspoon laos powder, optional
4 tablespoons oil
2 medium onions, finely chopped
2 cups (16 fl oz) thin coconut milk
2 daun salam *or* 6 curry leaves
1 stem lemon grass *or*
    3 strips thinly peeled lemon rind
5 cm (2 in) piece cinnamon stick
1½ cups (12 fl oz) thick coconut milk
1 tablespoon lemon juice *or* tamarind liquid
extra salt to taste

Divide chicken into serving pieces. In a small bowl, combine garlic, salt, pepper, ginger, nuts, coriander, cummin, fennel and laos if used. Mix to a paste, adding a little of the oil if necessary. Rub paste well into the pieces of chicken and leave for 1 hour.

Heat 2 tablespoons of the oil in a frying pan and fry sliced onion slowly until golden brown. Drain from oil and set aside. Add remaining oil to pan and fry the spiced chicken pieces gently, just until they start to colour. Add thin coconut milk, daun salam, lemon grass or rind and cinnamon stick. Stir until it comes to the boil, then cook uncovered for 30 minutes or until chicken is tender. Add thick coconut milk, stir thoroughly and cook for a further 15 minutes, uncovered. Remove from heat, add lemon juice and season to taste with extra salt. Remove whole spices. Garnish with fried onions and serve the chicken with white rice, vegetables and sambals.

SRI LANKA
CHICKEN CURRY

(Picture on opposite page)

Your Sri Lankan guest would shake his head with joyous approval if you dry roast the coriander, cummin and fennel to a rich brown before using them in this dish. **Reuben.**

Serves: 4-5

1.5 kg (3 lb) chicken *or* chicken pieces
3 tablespoons ghee *or* oil
¼ teaspoon fenugreek seeds, optional
10 curry leaves
2 large onions, finely chopped
2-2½ teaspoons finely chopped garlic
2 teaspoons finely grated fresh ginger
1 teaspoon ground turmeric
1 teaspoon chilli powder
1 tablespoon ground coriander
1 teaspoon ground cummin
½ teaspoon ground fennel
2 teaspoons paprika
2 teaspoons salt
2 tablespoons vinegar
2 tomatoes, peeled and chopped
6 cardamom pods, bruised
1 stick cinnamon
1 stem fresh lemon grass *or* 2 strips lemon rind
1 cup (8 fl oz) thick coconut milk

Joint chicken. Cut breast and thighs in halves, leave wings and drumsticks whole. Heat ghee and fry fenugreek and curry leaves until they start to brown. Add onions, garlic and ginger and fry gently until onions are quite soft and golden. Add turmeric, chilli, coriander, cummin, fennel, paprika, salt and vinegar. Stir well.

Add chicken and stir over medium heat until chicken is thoroughly coated with spices. Add tomatoes, whole spices and lemon grass and cook, covered, over low heat 40-50 minutes. Add coconut milk, taste and add more salt and a squeeze of lemon juice if desired. Do not cover after adding coconut milk. Serve with rice and accompaniments.

Note: Paprika is used to give the required red colour — in Sri Lanka the colour is achieved by using about 30 red chillies!

Chicken Curry, recipe on opposite page

Fried Pork Curry, recipe page 46

BURMA

CHICKEN CURRY WITH SHRIMP PASTE

(Picture page 1)

*Shrimp paste and chicken? Go ahead and try it —
you'll go back for more.* **Reuben.**

Serves: 4-6

1 kg (2 lb) chicken, jointed
2 medium onions, sliced
2 tablespoons light sesame oil *or* corn oil
2 teaspoons dried shrimp paste
1 teaspoon finely chopped garlic
1 teaspoon finely chopped fresh ginger
1 teaspoon ground turmeric
1 teaspoon chilli powder
2 teaspoons salt
½ cup (4 fl oz) hot water
squeeze of lemon juice

Garnish
¼ cup (½ oz) chopped coriander

Heat oil in a saucepan and brown onions on medium heat. Add shrimp paste, garlic and ginger, lower heat and stir for a few minutes. Add turmeric, chilli powder and salt, stir well and cook 1 minute longer. Add chicken and mix till well coated. Add water and bring to boil.

Turn heat low, cover and simmer until chicken is tender, stirring occasionally. Add lemon juice, sprinkle with chopped fresh coriander and serve with white rice.

INDIA

MADRAS CHICKEN CURRY

*Be warned. This is a really hot curry. Remember to
eat it with sufficient quantities of rice, and keep the
beer or water well within reach!* **Reuben.**

Serves: 6

1 x 1.5 kg (3 lb) roasting chicken
3 tablespoons oil
12 curry leaves
2 medium onions, finely chopped
2 teaspoons finely chopped garlic
2 teaspoons finely chopped fresh ginger
1 teaspoon ground turmeric
3 teaspoons chilli powder
3 teaspoons ground coriander
1 teaspoon ground cummin
2½ teaspoons salt
1 large, ripe tomato, peeled and chopped
2 small sticks cinnamon
2 cups (16 fl oz) coconut milk

Cut chicken into curry pieces (see page 70). Heat oil, fry curry leaves, onions, garlic and ginger until soft. Add turmeric, chilli powder, coriander, cummin and fry for 2 minutes. Add salt and tomato, stir well, cover and cook until tomato is pulpy. Add chicken and cinnamon sticks and stir well until chicken is coated with the spice mixture.

Cover and cook for 30 minutes, or until chicken is almost tender. Stir in the coconut milk and simmer, uncovered, for about 15 minutes longer. Serve with rice and accompaniments.

BURMA
CHICKEN CURRY WITH GRAVY

Serves: 4-6

1 x 1.5 kg (3 lb) chicken
2 medium onions
3 cloves garlic
1 teaspoon finely grated fresh ginger
1 stem lemon grass *or* 2 strips lemon rind
3 tablespoons vegetable oil
2 teaspoons salt *or* to taste
1 teaspoon turmeric
1 teaspoon chilli powder, optional
1 cup (8 fl oz) water
1 large ripe tomato, chopped
2 large potatoes, peeled and cubed *or*
    2 cups (3½ oz) cauliflower sprigs
1 tablespoon fish sauce
1 tablespoon tamarind liquid *or* lemon juice
1 tablespoon chopped fresh coriander leaves
¼ teaspoon ground cardamom

Proceed as for Chicken Curry Dry (following recipe). When chicken is half-cooked, add water, tomato, potato, fish sauce, and tamarind or lemon juice. Continue cooking until potato is done, stirring occasionally. If cauliflower if used in preference to potato, add it when chicken is nearly done. Finally add coriander leaves and cardamom. Stir and serve.

BURMA
CHICKEN CURRY, DRY

This dry curry is usually served with a garlic-prawn-based soup to moisten the rice. **Reuben.**

Serves: 4-6

1 x 1.5 kg (3 lb) chicken
2 medium onions
3 cloves garlic
1 teaspoon finely grated fresh ginger
1 stem lemon grass *or* 2 strips lemon rind
3 tablespoons vegetable oil
1½ teaspoons salt *or* to taste
1 teaspoon ground turmeric
½ teaspoon chilli powder, optional
¼ teaspoon ground cardamom
1 tablespoon chopped fresh coriander leaves

Cut chicken into curry pieces. Peel and roughly chop onions and put into blender container with garlic, ginger, sliced lemon grass or lemon rind. Add a little oil to facilitate blending and blend ingredients to a smooth pulp.

Heat remaining oil in a saucepan and when very hot add blended ingredients, salt, turmeric and chilli powder (if used) and fry over medium heat, stirring

well with a wooden spoon. Add a few drops of water if mixture starts to stick to base of pan. Simmer on low heat until the moisture content of the onions has evaporated and the ingredients turn a rich red-brown colour. At this stage they will begin to stick to the pan so keep stirring, and add the chicken pieces, turning them well in the mixture so that they are coated.

Cover and simmer for 35-45 minutes or until chicken is tender. The juices from the chicken will provide sufficient liquid for this curry, so do not add water or other liquid. As cooking is nearing completion, stir occasionally to prevent sticking. Add cardamom and coriander leaves, stir quickly and replace lid for a few seconds to hold in the aroma. Serve with white rice and other accompaniments.

THAILAND
CHICKEN WITH COCONUT MILK & LAOS

In South-East Asian countries, fresh laos, an aromatic rhizome, is a popular ingredient. In countries where it does not grow, a thumb-sized piece of laos is replaced by a few slices of dried laos, or the easier-to-use laos powder. **Charmaine.**

Serves: 5

6 slices fresh or dried laos *or* 4 teaspoons laos
    powder
1 roasting chicken, about 1.25 kg (2½ lb)
2½ cups (20 fl oz) thin coconut milk
½ teaspoon black pepper
2-3 fresh coriander roots, crushed
6 strips thinly peeled lemon rind
3 fresh green chillies
1½ teaspoons salt
3 fresh leaves from lemon *or* other
    citrus tree
1 cup (8 fl oz) thick coconut milk
1 tablespoon fish sauce
lemon juice to taste
3 tablespoons finely chopped fresh
    coriander leaves

Soak the dried laos in hot water for 30 minutes and pulverize in blender with some of the liquid. Cut chicken into serving pieces and put into saucepan with thin coconut milk, laos, pepper, coriander roots, lemon rind, chillies (whole), salt and citrus leaves. Bring slowly to the boil and simmer, uncovered, until chicken is tender, stirring occasionally. Add thick coconut milk and stir constantly until it returns to the boil.

Remove from heat and stir in the fish sauce and lemon juice. Serve in a deep dish or bowl with chopped coriander leaves on top. Accompany with white rice.

INDIA
CHICKEN VINDALOO

The vinegar and spices used in this preparation allow the chicken to be kept for weeks — if you can resist it for so long! **Reuben.**

Serves: 6

1 x 2 kg (4 lb) roasting chicken
2 tablespoons cummin seed
1 tablespoon black mustard seed
3 teaspoons chilli powder *or* to taste
1 tablespoon chopped ginger
1 tablespoon chopped garlic
¾ cup (6 fl oz) vinegar
1 teaspoon ground cinnamon
¼ teaspoon ground cloves
¼ teaspoon ground cardamom
4 tablespoons oil
2 teaspoons salt
½ teaspoon ground black pepper

Cut the chicken into curry pieces (see page 70). Grind the cummin seeds, mustard seeds, ginger and garlic in electric blender with the vinegar. Use high speed so that mixture is finely ground. Add the ground spices.

Heat oil in a heavy saucepan, remove from heat and add the ground mixture to the hot oil. Stir for a few seconds, then add the chicken pieces and stir again so that each piece is coated with the spices. Let it stand for an hour or longer.

Return to low heat and bring to simmering point, add salt and black pepper and simmer, covered, until chicken is tender. Stir from time to time so that spices do not stick at base of pan. Serve with plain white rice.

INDIA
CHICKEN SHAGUTI

We first tasted this dish in Bombay. This spice combination is also popular in other parts of India. **Charmaine.**

Serves: 6

1 x 1.5 kg (3 lb) roasting chicken
8 dried red chillies
1 tablespoon ground coriander
1 teaspoon ground cummin
½ teaspoon fenugreek seeds
8 whole black peppercorns
3 teaspoons white poppy seeds *or* ground almonds
½ cup (2 oz) desiccated coconut
1 large onion, finely sliced
2 teaspoons chopped fresh ginger
2 teaspoons chopped garlic
½ teaspoon ground cardamom
¼ teaspoon ground cloves
½ teaspoon ground cinnamon
2 teaspoons salt
1 tablespoon ghee
2 tablespoons oil
1 teaspoon ground turmeric
juice of half a lemon

Cut chicken into curry pieces. Remove stalks and seeds from chillies and soak the chillies in hot water for 10 minutes. Meanwhile, roast coriander and cummin in a dry pan over medium heat for a minute or two, until the colour changes and a pleasant aroma is given off. Turn on to a plate. Roast fenugreek seeds and peppercorns for 2 or 3 minutes, stirring constantly or shaking pan. In the same way roast the poppy seeds and the desiccated coconut, separately. Add to the other roasted spices. Put the sliced onion in the pan and dry roast, stirring, until brown.

Put chillies into jar of electric blender with all the roasted ingredients and the turmeric, cardamom, cloves and cinnamon. Add some of the water in which the chillies were soaked and grind to a paste.

Heat ghee and oil in a heavy pan and fry the ground mixture and the ginger and garlic, stirring constantly, until oil separates from the mass. Put in the chicken, sprinkle with salt and stir to coat every piece of chicken with the spices.

Add ½ cup hot water, cover and cook on very low heat, stirring occasionally and adding more water if necessary, until the chicken is tender. Add lemon juice when chicken is cooked. The gravy should be very thick and dark. Serve with rice and accompaniments, such as Onion and Tomato Sambal (page 104) and Beetroot Raita (page 108).

MALAYSIA
CHICKEN CURRY WITH TOASTED COCONUT

Toasting the coconut imparts a rich brown colour and distinctive flavour to this curry. **Charmaine.**

Serves: 6

1 x 1.5 kg (3 lb) roasting chicken
4-6 fresh red chillies
½ cup (1½ oz) desiccated coconut
2 cups (16 fl oz) thick coconut milk
2 onions, roughly chopped
3 cloves garlic
1 teaspoon dried shrimp paste
1 teaspoon ground turmeric
1 tablespoon ground coriander
2 teaspoons ground cummin
1 stem fresh lemon grass *or* 2 strips lemon rind
3 tablespoons peanut oil
2 teaspoons salt
4 daun salam *or* 6 curry leaves
2 teaspoons laos powder

Cut chicken into joints. Drain. Remove chilli seeds if you don't want a very hot curry.

Put desiccated coconut into a heavy frying pan and fry on medium heat, stirring constantly, until it becomes a rich, dark brown. Immediately turn it on to a plate, for it will burn if left in the pan. When coconut has cooled slightly put it into the container of an electric blender, grind finely, then add about half a cup (4 fl oz) of the coconut milk and blend again on high speed for 1 minute. (In Asia fresh coconut would be roasted over coals and the nut meat then ground to a paste on a grinding stone, but in Western kitchens other means must be found.)

Set the coconut mixture aside in a bowl and, without washing blender container, put in the chillies, onions, garlic, dried shrimp paste, turmeric, coriander, cummin and sliced lemon grass or lemon rind. Blend to a purée. The water content of the onions should be enough to turn the mixture to a purée but if necessary add a tablespoon of the peanut oil.

Heat remaining oil in a large saucepan and fry the onion mixture on low heat, stirring constantly, until moisture evaporates and oil shows around edge. Add ground coconut, coconut milk, salt, daun salam and laos powder and stir well. Add chicken and stir gently as mixture comes to simmering point. Simmer, uncovered, for 1 hour or until chicken is tender, stirring occasionally. Serve with rice and other accompaniments.

INDIA
HUNDRED ALMOND CURRY

Sounds extravagant? Well, why not. Who should count pennies when creating a masterpiece? **Reuben.**

Serves: 6

1 x 1.75 kg (3½ lb) roasting chicken *or*
  1 kg (2 lb) boneless lamb
5 medium onions
2 tablespoons ghee
2 tablespoons oil
3 teaspoons finely chopped garlic
3 teaspoons finely grated fresh ginger
1 tablespoon ground coriander
1 tablespoon ground cummin
1 teaspoon ground turmeric
½ teaspoon ground fennel
1 teaspoon chilli powder, optional
3 teaspoons salt
3 large ripe tomatoes, peeled and chopped
¼ cup (½ oz) chopped fresh coriander or mint leaves
100 blanched almonds (about 125 g)
oil for frying
1 cup (8 fl oz) natural yoghurt
1 teaspoon garam masala (see page 14)

Cut chicken into curry pieces or lamb into large cubes. Peel onions, chop 3 onions finely and slice the remaining two very fine. Heat ghee and oil in a large heavy saucepan and fry the sliced onion, stirring, until it is golden brown. Remove from pan and set aside. Add the chopped onion, garlic and ginger to the oil left in pan and fry on low heat, stirring occasionally, until very soft and turning golden. Long, slow cooking at this stage is essential if the curry is to have good flavour.

Add the coriander, cummin, turmeric, fennel and chilli powder and fry, stirring, for a minute or two. Add salt, tomatoes and half the fresh herbs, stir well and cook until tomatoes are pulpy. Cover pan to hasten this process, but uncover and stir now and then to ensure mixture does not stick at base of pan.

Put in the chicken pieces and stir well so that each piece is coated with the mixture. Cover pan and cook on very low heat for 40 minutes or until chicken is tender. Meanwhile, heat oil and fry half the almonds until golden. In electric blender grind remaining almonds. Beat the yoghurt with a fork until it is quite smooth and stir into the curry together with the fried almonds. Simmer 5 minutes, uncovered. Stir in the garam masala, reserved fried onions, ground almonds and remaining chopped herbs. Heat through and serve.

CHICKEN CURRY WITH NOODLES

(Picture page 79)

Serve noodles in a large bowl and the curry in a separate bowl. Each person takes a serving of noodles, ladles on a generous amount of the curry and sprinkles various accompaniments over the top. **Charmaine.**

Serves: 6-8

1.5 kg (3 lb) chicken *or* chicken pieces
5 cloves garlic
3 medium onions, chopped
1 tablespoon finely chopped fresh ginger
1 teaspoon dried shrimp paste
2 tablespoons peanut oil
1 tablespoon sesame oil
1-2 teaspoons chilli powder
2 teaspoons salt
2 cups (16 fl oz) thin coconut milk
2 cups (16 fl oz) thick coconut milk
2 tablespoons chick pea flour
500 g (1 lb) thin egg noodles *or*
    cellophane noodles

Cut chicken into serving pieces. Put garlic, onion, ginger and dried shrimp paste into blender container, cover and blend until smooth, adding 1 tablespoon of peanut oil if necessary. Heat remaining oil and fry blended ingredients for 5 minutes. Add chicken and continue to fry, stirring constantly. Add chilli powder, salt and thin coconut milk. Simmer until chicken is tender, adding a little hot water if mixture becomes too dry.

Add thick coconut milk, return to heat and bring slowly to the boil, stirring constantly to prevent mixture from curdling. Mix chick pea flour with a little cold water to a smooth cream, add to curry and cook for a further 5 minutes uncovered (there should be a lot of gravy). If preparing curry a day or two beforehand, refrigerate immediately and reheat when required.

Just before serving, cook noodles in a large saucepan of boiling salted water until just tender, about 6 minutes. Pour cold water into pan to stop noodles cooking, then drain in colander.

Accompaniments:
finely sliced spring onions, both green and white
    portions
chopped fresh coriander leaves
finely sliced white onion
roasted chick peas, finely ground in a blender *or*
    crushed with mortar and pestle
crisp fried noodles, broken into small pieces
fried onion flakes
thin slices garlic, fried in oil until golden
lemon wedges

dried chillies, fried in oil 3-4 seconds
chilli powder

Note: **Roasted chick peas are sold in Greek delicatessen shops.**

JAVANESE CHICKEN CURRY

A fragrant, lightly spiced dish. Without the chillies it is ideal for children. **Charmaine.**

Serves: 4-6

1 x 1.5 kg (3 lb) roasting chicken
1 medium onion, chopped
1 teaspoon finely chopped garlic
1 teaspoon chopped fresh ginger
3 fresh red chillies *or* 1 teaspoon sambal ulek
2 candle nuts *or* Brazil nuts
¾ cup (6 fl oz) coconut milk
1 tablespoon desiccated or fresh grated coconut
2 teaspoons ground coriander
1 teaspoon laos powder, optional
½ teasoon ground tumeric
1½ teaspoons salt
1 stem fresh lemon grass, *or*
    3 strips thinly peeled lemon rind
2 daun salam *or* 6 curry leaves

Cut chicken into curry pieces (see page 70).

Put onion, garlic, ginger, chillies and nuts in blender container with half the coconut milk and the desiccated coconut. Cover and blend on high speed for approximately 30 seconds or until smooth. Rinse blender container with remaining coconut milk and add to pan. Add all remaining ingredients, and bring slowly to the boil, stirring. Cook, uncovered, until chicken is tender and gravy thick and almost dry.

Serve with white rice and a sayur (vegetable cooked in coconut milk) or a curry with plenty of gravy.

CHICKEN & BAMBOO SHOOT CURRY

The contrasting textures of bamboo shoot and chicken produce a very unusual curry. **Charmaine.**

Serves: 6-8

1 x 1.5 kg (3 lb) roasting chicken
1 can bamboo shoots
2 medium onions
4 tablespoons coconut *or* peanut oil
1½ tablespoons ground coriander
1 teaspoon dried shrimp paste
1 teaspoon laos powder
1 teaspoon chilli powder
2 teaspoons salt
2 cups (16 fl oz) thin coconut milk
1 cup (8 fl oz) thick coconut milk

Cut chicken into curry pieces. Drain bamboo shoots and cut into quarters, then into slices. Chop onions finely. Heat the oil in a large saucepan and fry onions over medium heat, stirring, until soft and golden. Add coriander, dried shrimp paste, laos, chilli powder and salt and fry, stirring constantly, for a few minutes until spices are brown.

Add chicken pieces and stir until well mixed with the spices, then add thin coconut milk and bring to simmering point. Simmer for 20-25 minutes. Add bamboo shoot, stir, and simmer for a further 20 minutes or until chicken is tender. Add thick coconut milk and simmer, uncovered, stirring gently. Taste and add salt if necessary. Continue simmering until oil rises to the surface. Serve with rice, vegetables and sambal.

CHICKEN WHITE CURRY

Fresh dill seems so Scandinavian, but it is a popular herb in certain dishes in Sri Lanka. Try it also in meatballs and fish cakes. **Charmaine.**

Serves: 4-6

1.5 kg (3 lb) chicken, jointed
1 tablespoon chopped fresh dill weed
1 teaspoon chopped garlic
1 teaspoon chopped fresh ginger
½ teaspoon ground turmeric
2 teaspoons salt
2 teaspoons chilli powder
1 tablespoon ground coriander
1 teaspoon ground cummin
½ teaspoon ground fennel
¼ teaspoon fenugreek seeds
1 stick cinnamon
2 stems fresh lemon grass, bruised
12 curry leaves
2 medium onions, finely sliced
2 cups (16 fl oz) thick coconut milk
hot water
1 tablespoon ghee *or* oil
2 teaspoons black mustard seeds

Place chicken in a saucepan with dill weed, garlic, ginger, turmeric, salt, chilli powder, coriander, cummin, fennel, fenugreek, cinnamon and lemon grass. Also add half the curry leaves, one sliced onion, half the coconut milk and sufficient hot water to cover the chicken pieces. Bring to a rapid boil, lower heat, cover and simmer for 20 minutes, stirring occasionally.

In another saucepan heat the ghee, add the remaining curry leaves, remaining sliced onion and mustard seeds. Stir-fry till onions are soft and golden, then stir in remaining coconut milk. Add this mixture to saucepan containing the chicken, stir well and cook further 10 minutes or until chicken is tender. Serve with rice and accompaniments.

MALAYSIA
HOT CHICKEN CURRY

Serves: 6

1.5 kg (3 lb) chicken, jointed
1 tablespoon ground coriander
1 teaspoon ground fennel
1 teaspoon ground black pepper
5 candle nuts *or* 4 Brazil kernels, chopped
8 dried red chillies
1 teaspoon chopped garlic
½ teaspoon ground turmeric
½ teaspoon ground cinnamon
1 stem fresh lemon grass, finely sliced *or*
    rind of half a lemon
1 teaspoon laos powder
2 teaspoons salt
3 tablespoons peanut oil
3 medium onions, finely sliced
3 fresh red chillies, sliced
hot water
½ cup (4 fl oz) coconut milk

Place in container of electric blender the coriander, fennel, pepper, chopped nuts, chillies, garlic, turmeric, cinnamon, lemon grass, laos and salt. Blend to a fine paste, adding a little water to facilitate blending.

Heat oil in a large saucepan and fry onions till soft and golden. Add blended mixture and cook stirring, till oil comes to the surface and mixture smells aromatic. Add chicken pieces and sliced chillies and cook, stirring for 5 minutes. Lower heat and cook covered till chicken is tender, stirring occasionally, and adding a little hot water to prevent sticking. Stir in coconut milk, simmer further 5 minutes and serve with rice and accompaniments.

INDIA
CURRIED CHICKEN LIVERS

Many and varied are the ways in which chicken liver is used in India. Spiced and barbecued for kebabs, or dry chilli-fried with drinks. This recipe is yet another way of serving them. **Reuben.**

Serves: 4-5

500 g (1 lb) chicken livers
2 tablespoons ghee *or* oil
2 medium onions, finely chopped
1 teaspoon finely grated garlic
2 teaspoons finely grated fresh ginger
½ teaspoon ground turmeric
½ teaspoon chilli powder
1 tablespoon ground coriander
2 teaspoons ground cummin
2 ripe tomatoes, peeled and chopped
1 teaspoon salt
1 teaspoon garam masala

Wash the livers and drain in a colander. Cut them in halves and if there are any yellow spots on the livers slice them off with a sharp knife. Heat the ghee or oil in a heavy saucepan and fry the onion, stirring occasionally, until soft. Add the garlic and ginger and continue frying until golden.

Add tumeric, chilli powder, coriander and cummin. Fry for 2 minutes, stirring, then add the tomatoes and salt and cook, covered, on low heat until tomatoes are puréed, stirring occasionally. Add the chicken livers and stir gently. Replace lid and cook for 15 minutes, sprinkle garam masala over and simmer for a minute or two. Serve hot with rice and other accompaniments.

SRI LANKA
CHICKEN GIZZARD CURRY

If you haven't had curried giblets before, why not? It's the 'in' thing. **Reuben.**

Serves: 6

750 g (1½ lb) chicken gizzards
1½ tablespoons ground coriander
3 teaspoons ground cummin
4 tablespoons oil *or* ghee
2 medium onions, finely chopped
2½ teaspoons finely chopped garlic
1 tablespoon finely chopped fresh ginger
1 teaspoon chilli powder
½ teaspoon ground turmeric
½ teaspoon ground fenugreek, optional
2 ripe tomatoes, chopped
1½ teaspoons salt
2 tablespoons chopped fresh coriander leaves

Wash and clean the gizzards well, leave to drain in colander. Put the ground coriander in a small dry pan and stir over low heat for a few minutes until roasted to a fairly dark brown and spreading a pleasant aroma. Turn the coriander on to a plate. Roast the cummin in the same way.

Heat the oil in a large heavy saucepan. When hot, put in onions, garlic and ginger. Fry, stirring, until onions are soft and start to turn golden brown. Add the chilli powder, turmeric, fenugreek and the previously roasted coriander and cummin. Cook, stirring, for 1 minute, then add the tomatoes and salt and stir well. Add the chicken gizzards and stir until they are well coated with spice mixture. Add hot water to cover and simmer for 1 hour or until gizzards are tender. Sprinkle with coriander leaves, stir and cook for 5 minutes longer. Serve hot with rice.

THAILAND
MOSLEM CHICKEN CURRY

Serves: 6-8

1 roasting chicken about 1.75 kg (3½ lb)
4 cups (32 fl oz) coconut milk
1 cup (5 oz) roasted, unsalted peanuts
2 tablespoons fish sauce
15 cardamom pods
1 stick cinnamon, about 5 cm (2 in)
1 quantity Moslem curry paste (see page 18)
3 tablespoons tamarind liquid
2 tablespoons lime *or* lemon juice
1-2 tablespoons sugar
extra fish sauce if necessary

Cut chicken into curry pieces (see page 70). Put into a saucepan with the coconut milk, peanuts, fish sauce, cardamom pods and cinnamon. Bring slowly to simmering point, stirring frequently with a wooden spoon. Turn heat low and allow to simmer, uncovered, until meat is tender. This should take about 35-40 minutes. Do not cover at any stage or the coconut milk will curdle. Stir occasionally during this initial cooking.

Meanwhile, make the curry paste. When the chicken is just tender lift it out and simmer the coconut milk a little longer, until it is reduced by about a third. If it has already reduced considerably, do not give it this further cooking. Stir in the curry paste, tamarind liquid, lemon juice and sugar. Return chicken to pan and continue simmering until the gravy is thickened slightly. Taste and add more fish sauce if necessary. Serve with white rice.

INDIA
CHICKEN & YOGHURT CURRY

The tangy flavour of the yoghurt blends with and complements the spices used in this recipe. **Reuben.**

Serves: 4

1 kg (2 lb) roasting chicken
1 medium onion, roughly chopped
3 cloves garlic, peeled
1 teaspoon finely chopped fresh ginger
½ cup (2 oz) fresh coriander or mint leaves
1½ tablespoons ghee *or* oil
1 teaspoon ground turmeric
1½ teaspoons garam masala (see page 14)
1½ teaspoons salt
½ teaspoon chilli powder, optional
½ cup (4 fl oz) natural yoghurt
2 ripe tomatoes, diced

Garnish
extra chopped mint *or* coriander leaves.

Cut chicken into serving pieces, or use chicken pieces of one kind — drumsticks, thighs or half breasts.

Put into container of electric blender the onion, garlic, ginger, fresh coriander or mint. Blend to a smooth purée. Heat oil in a heavy saucepan and fry the blended mixture, stirring, for about 5 minutes. Add turmeric, garam masala, salt and chilli powder and fry for a further minute. Stir in yoghurt and tomatoes, and fry until liquid dries up and the mixture is the consistency of thick purée.

Add chicken pieces, turning them in the spice mixture so they are coated on both sides, then turn heat low, cover tightly and cook until chicken is tender. If liquid from chicken has not evaporated by the time the flesh is cooked, uncover and raise heat to dry off excess liquid, stirring gently at the base of pan to prevent burning. Garnish with chopped herbs and serve with rice or chapatis.

INDIA
CHICKEN DOPIAZA

Serves: 6

1 x 1.5 kg (3 lb) roasting chicken
6 medium onions
4 fresh green chillies, seeded
4 teaspoons chopped garlic
1½ tablespoons finely grated fresh ginger
1 tablespoon ground coriander
1 tablespoon ground cummin
2 teaspoons ground turmeric
1 teaspoon ground cinnamon
1 tablespoon ground cardamon
¼ teaspoon ground cloves
6 tablespoons ghee *or* oil
3 ripe tomatoes, peeled and chopped
3 teaspoons salt
1 cup (8 fl oz) water

Cut chicken into curry pieces. Thinly slice half the onions and set aside. Roughly chop the rest of the onions and put into container of electric blender with the chillies, garlic and ginger. Blend to a puree. Mix in the ground spices, coriander, cummin, turmeric, cinnamon, cardamon and cloves.

Heat ghee or oil in a large saucepan and fry the sliced onions, stirring frequently, until they are golden brown. Remove onions from pan with slotted spoon. Add the ground mixture to oil remaining in pan and fry, stirring, until colour darkens and oil appears around the edges. Add tomatoes, stir and cook until liquid from tomatoes is almost evaporated. Add the chicken pieces and stir well. Add water and salt, cover and cook for 35 minutes or until chicken is tender. Add reserved fried onions, cover and simmer 5 minutes longer. Serve with rice or parathas.

SRI LANKA
DUCK CURRY, DRY

This is a very rich curry that should be offset by plain white rice and other lighter curries such as a white vegetable curry. Piquant accompaniments such as pickled lime sambol and a fresh cucumber and onion salad also go well with it. **Charmaine**

Serves: 4-5

1.5 kg (3 lb) duck, jointed
2 large onions, chopped
3 teaspoons chopped garlic
1½ tablespoons finely chopped fresh ginger
2 tablespoons Ceylon curry powder (see page 17)
1 stick cinnamon
8 strips rampé leaf (pandanus)
1 stem fresh lemon grass *or*
    rind of half a lemon
3 cups (24 fl oz) coconut milk
2 teaspoons salt
¼ cup (2 fl oz) vinegar
1 tablespoon brown sugar
2 tablespoons ghee *or* oil

Joint duck and place into a large heavy saucepan with all the ingredients except sugar and ghee. Bring to the boil, then cover and simmer until duck is tender.

Heat ghee in another pan and fry the pieces of duck, then pour in the gravy, add sugar and simmer a further 10 minutes. Serve with rice and accompaniments.

MALAYSIA
DUCK CURRY, DRY

Serves: 4-5

1.5 kg (3 lb) duck, jointed
3 medium onions, roughly chopped
5 candle nuts *or*
    4 Brazil kernels, chopped
6 dried red chillies
½ teaspoon turmeric
1 teaspoon dried shrimp paste
1 teaspoon ground cardamom
½ teaspoon ground cinnamon
½ teaspoon ground cloves
1 teaspoon laos powder
2 teaspoons salt
3 tablespoons peanut oil
1 tablespoon curry leaves
¼ cup (2 fl oz) coconut milk
hot water

Place in container of electric blender the onions, Brazil kernels, chillies, turmeric, dried shrimp paste, cardamom, cinnamon, cloves, laos and salt. Blend to a fine paste, adding a little water to facilitate blending.

Heat oil in a large saucepan. Add curry leaves and the blended mixture and cook, stirring, till oil comes to the surface and the mixture smells aromatic. Stir in the duck pieces and cook for 5 minutes. Lower heat and simmer covered till duck is tender, stirring occasionally, and adding a little hot water to prevent sticking. Stir in coconut milk and cook uncovered till gravy thickens. Serve with rice and accompaniments.

THAILAND
GREEN CURRY OF DUCK

The green colour is imparted by the finely chopped chillies and fresh herbs added during the last few minutes of cooking. These two ingredients not only give colour, but also a distinctive flavour that distinguishes Thai dishes from other spiced preparations with a coconut milk gravy. Please note that canned coconut milk cannot be used in this recipe.

Serves: 4

1 roasting duck, 1.5 kg (3 lb)
3½-4 cups (28-32 fl oz) coconut milk (see page 9)
3 tablespoons green curry paste (see page 15)
2 sprigs tender citrus leaves
1 teaspoon salt
2 tablespoons fish sauce
2 tablespoons finely chopped fresh green
    chillies, seeds removed
4 tablespoons finely chopped fresh basil *or*
    coriander leaves

Divide duck into joints. Make coconut milk as instructed on page 9 and put the first extract or thick milk in the refrigerator or in a cool place for an hour or so until the cream rises to the top. Spoon off the cream or richest part of the milk into a cup. Heat this cupful of coconut cream in a large heavy saucepan, stirring constantly until it comes to the boil. Lower heat and continue cooking, stirring occasionally, until the cream thickens and oil bubbles around it. By this time it should be reduced to a quarter of the original amount. Add the curry paste and fry the rich oily cream for about 5 minutes, stirring constantly. The curry paste will smell cooked and oil will separate from it when it is ready.

When this happens add the pieces of duck and cook over medium low heat stirring frequently and turning them, for about 15 minutes. The duck will change colour and have a cooked appearance. Add the remaining coconut milk, citrus leaves, salt and fish sauce and stir while the coconut milk comes to the boil. Then turn heat low and allow to simmer uncovered for 35-45 minutes or until the duck is well cooked and tender and the gravy rich and oily. (In Thai curries, the aim is *not* to reduce the liquid to a small amount of thick, almost dry curry, so add extra coconut milk if necessary.) Stir in the chopped fresh chillies and herbs, simmer for 5 minutes longer, then turn into serving dish. Serve with white rice.

INDONESIA
PADANG DUCK CURRY

Serves: 4-5

1.5 kg (3 lb) duck, jointed
3 daun salam *or* 6 curry leaves
2 cups (16 fl oz) thick coconut milk
3 medium onions, roughly chopped
1 teaspoon laos powder
2 teaspoons chopped garlic
1 teaspoon chopped fresh ginger
½ teaspoon dried shrimp paste
1 teaspoon ground turmeric
4 dried red chillies
1 stem fresh lemon grass, finely sliced *or*
    rind of ½ lemon
5 candle nuts *or* 4 Brazil kernels, chopped
2 teaspoons salt
2 teaspoons tamarind paste
½ cup hot water

Place in container of electric blender the onions, laos, garlic, ginger, shrimp paste, turmeric, chillies, lemon grass and candle nut kernels. Blend to a fine paste, adding a little hot water to facilitate blending.

Put duck, daun salam and coconut milk in a saucepan, add blended ingredients and bring to the boil. Add the salt and tamarind paste dissolved in hot water, reduce heat and simmer, stirring frequently, until coconut milk is absorbed and the oil comes to the surface. Add sufficient hot water to prevent sticking, stir and cook until duck is tender. Serve with rice.

DUCK VINDALOO

I would use the chilli seeds for a really hot, tangy dish. **Reuben.**

I would remove the seeds unless cooking for confirmed chilli freaks. **Charmaine.**

Serves: 4-5

1 x 1.5 kg (3 lb) duck
10 dried red chillies
½ cup (4 fl oz) vinegar
1 tablespoon chopped garlic
1 tablespoon chopped fresh ginger
1 tablespoon ground coriander
2 teaspoons ground cummin
1 teaspoon ground turmeric
½ teaspoon ground black pepper
2-3 tablespoons ghee *or* oil
2 teaspoons salt
1 tablespoon sugar

Cut the duck into joints. Remove stalks and seeds from dried chillies and soak in vinegar for about 10 minutes. Put chillies, vinegar, garlic and ginger into container of electric blender and blend until smooth. Scrape mixture out of blender jar into a large bowl and mix in the ground spices. Add pieces of duck, turn them over in the mixture until they are well coated, cover and leave for 2 hours at room temperature or overnight in the refrigerator.

In a large saucepan heat the ghee or oil and fry the pieces of duck lightly. Add salt and a little hot water together with any marinade left. Cover and simmer on low heat until duck is tender, adding a little more water if necessary during cooking. At end of cooking time stir in the sugar. Serve with rice.

OMELETTE CURRY

Serves: 4

Omelettes
6 eggs
1 small onion, finely chopped
1 fresh green chilli, seeded and finely chopped
2 teaspoons fresh dill, finely chopped *or*
    ½ teaspoon dried dill weed
salt and pepper to taste
ghee *or* butter

Gravy
3 cups (24 fl oz) thin coconut milk
1 medium onion, finely sliced
2 fresh chillies, seeded and split
½ teaspoon ground turmeric
1 teaspoon finely sliced garlic
½ teaspoon finely grated fresh ginger
1 stick cinnamon
4 dried rampé leaves
2 stems fresh lemon grass, bruised
8 curry leaves
salt to taste
1 cup (8 fl oz) thick coconut milk

Omelettes: Beat eggs together, add onion, chilli, dill, salt and pepper. Heat a little ghee in a frying pan and make 2 omelettes with mixture. Cut each omelette in 3 pieces. Heat through in prepared gravy and serve with boiled rice and accompaniments.

Gravy: Place all ingredients, except thick coconut milk, in a large saucepan and simmer gently, uncovered, for approximately 10 minutes. Add thick coconut milk, stir and simmer 5 minutes longer.

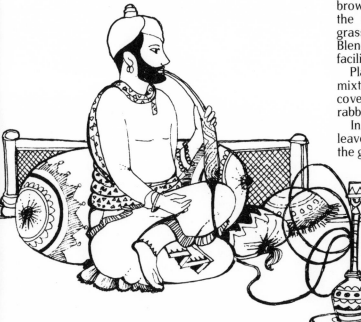

EGG CURRY

So you can't handle a hot curry? Try this — sans chilli powder. **Reuben.**

Serves: 4-6

6 eggs
2 tablespoons ghee *or* oil
2 medium onions, finely chopped
1½ teaspoons finely chopped garlic
2 teaspoons finely grated fresh ginger
3 teaspoons ground coriander
2 teaspoons ground cummin
1 teaspoon ground turmeric
½ teaspoon chilli powder
2-3 ripe tomatoes, diced
1 teaspoon salt *or* to taste
½ cup hot water
½ teaspoon garam masala (see page 14)

Hard boil the eggs, cool quickly under running cold tap, then shell and set aside. Heat ghee or oil and fry onions, garlic and ginger until soft and golden brown. Add coriander, cummin, turmeric and chilli and fry for a few seconds, then add tomatoes and salt and stir over medium heat until tomatoes are soft and pulpy.

Add hot water, cover and simmer until gravy is thick, then stir in garam masala and the halved eggs and heat through. Serve with rice.

RABBIT CURRY

Venison, peafowl, hare, snipe, teal are the game available in Sri Lanka, but I suggest rabbit in place of these more exotic creatures. They also make a similar curry using iguana which, I am told, could be mistaken for chicken. No, I haven't tasted it and I hope I never do! **Charmaine.**

I have, it's great! **Reuben.**

Serves: 4-5

1.5 kg (3 lb) rabbit, jointed
1 tablespoon ground coriander
1 teaspoon ground cummin
1 teaspoon ground fennel
8 dried red chillies
1 large onion, roughly chopped
2 teaspoons chopped garlic
2 teaspoons chopped fresh ginger
1 teaspoon ground turmeric
1 stem fresh lemon grass, chopped *or*
    rind of half lemon
1 teaspoon ground cardamom
1 teaspoon ground cinnamon
½ teaspoon ground cloves
2 teaspoons salt
2 tablespoons vinegar
hot water
1 cup (8 fl oz) thick coconut milk
8 curry leaves
1 tablespoon ghee *or* oil

Dry roast coriander, cummin and fennel to a golden brown. Place in the container of electric blender with the chillies, onion, garlic, ginger, turmeric, lemon grass, cardamom, cinnamon, cloves, salt and vinegar. Blend to a smooth paste, adding a little hot water to facilitate blending.

Place rabbit pieces in a saucepan, add the blended mixture, coconut milk and sufficient hot water to cover. Bring to a fast boil, lower heat and simmer until rabbit is tender and the gravy reduced.

In another saucepan heat the ghee, add the curry leaves and rabbit pieces. Stir fry for 2 minutes then add the gravy to it. Serve with rice and accompaniments.

vegetables

Many millions of Asians live on a pure vegetarian diet. This is especially true in India. In this chapter there are therefore many recipes from India, where fresh vegetables are combined with dried beans or lentils, or with fresh homemade cheese. This is the protein that balances the Indian diet.

In Asia, vegetables are never boiled in water and the water thrown away — that would be looked upon as foolishness, as indeed it is. Judiciously spiced and seasoned, vegetables are made so delicious that they could be relished as the only accompaniment to rice and chapati even by those who are not totally vegetarian.

Use the recipes in this section as a guide, then adapt them to whatever vegetables are in season and create interesting combinations of your own.

INDIA
BEAN & CABBAGE FOOGATH

(Picture on opposite page)

This is Charmaine's. She has a touch of magic with vegetables. **Reuben.**

Serves: 6

**250 g (8 oz) green beans
half a small cabbage
4 tablespoons oil
1 large onion, finely chopped
2 fresh green chillies, sliced (optional)
1 teaspoon finely chopped fresh ginger
1 teaspoon ground turmeric
1½ teaspoons salt, *or* to taste
3 tablespoons desiccated coconut**

Top and tail beans and cut into diagonal slices. Finely shred the cabbage. In a large saucepan heat oil and fry the onion, chillies and ginger until golden. Add turmeric, then toss in the vegetables and mix over low heat until vegetables are tender but still crisp. Sprinkle salt, mix well. Add coconut and toss over heat until any liquid is absorbed. Serve with rice or chapatis.

INDIA
CAULIFLOWER CURRY

(Picture on opposite page)

This is a good example of a 'dry curry' and the mundane cauliflower never tasted so good.
Charmaine

Serves: 4-6

**half a large cauliflower
4 tablespoons oil
1 teaspoon black mustard seeds
1 onion, finely chopped
1 teaspoon finely chopped garlic
1 teaspoon finely chopped fresh ginger
1 teaspoon ground turmeric
½ teaspoon chilli powder, optional
1½ teaspoons salt *or* to taste**

Separate cauliflower into sprigs, leaving some of the stalk on each. Heat the oil in a karhai (or wok) or large saucepan and fry the mustard seeds until they pop. Add the onion, garlic and ginger and fry until soft. Add turmeric, chilli powder and salt and stir well, then toss the cauliflower in the mixture so that all the pieces are tinged with yellow. Add ½ cup (4 fl oz) water, cover pan and simmer for 10-15 minutes or until cauliflower is tender but not mushy. Taste and add more salt if necessary and serve with rice.

A vegetarian thali meal. Rice, the staple food, is served with dhal, a favourite lentil purée, recipe page 99; Bean and Cabbage Foogath, recipe on opposite page; Cauliflower Curry, recipe on opposite page; Potato Curry, recipe page 95; and accompaniments like natural yoghurt, mango pickle and Coconut Chutney, recipe page 111.

Familiar vegetables prepared in delicious ways. Yellow Pumpkin Curry; Nepalese pea and Potato Curry; and Bean Sayur; all the recipes on opposite page.

INDONESIA
BEAN SAYUR

(Picture on opposite page)

Serves: 6

2 tablespoons peanut oil
1 onion, finely chopped
1 teaspoon finely chopped garlic
2 fresh red chillies, seeded and chopped
1 teaspoon dried shrimp paste
1 teaspoon finely grated lemon rind
2 teaspoons ground coriander
1 teaspoon ground cummin
½ teaspoon laos powder
1 teaspoon salt
2 tablespoons tamarind liquid *or* lemon juice
1 daun salam *or* 3 curry leaves
3 cups chicken stock
500 g (1 lb) fresh green beans, sliced
1 cooked chicken breast, skinned, boned and diced
1½ cups (12 fl oz) coconut milk

Heat oil, fry onion, garlic, chillies and dried shrimp paste for 5 minutes over medium heat, stirring and crushing shrimp paste with back of spoon. Add lemon rind and ground spices, fry 1 minute. Add salt, tamarind liquid, daun salam or curry leaves, stock and beans. Bring to the boil, simmer for 8 minutes. Add chicken and coconut milk. Simmer 5 minutes and serve.

Note: Rice vermicelli can be added to this sayur when it is the main dish. Soak 125 g (4 oz) of rice vermicelli in very hot water for 10 minutes, and drain well. Add to sayur and cook for further 2 minutes.

NEPAL
NEPALESE PEA & POTATO CURRY

(Picture on opposite page)

Serves: 4

3 tablespoons ghee and oil mixture
1 large onion, finely sliced
½ teaspoon ground black pepper
3 green chillies, chopped
2 teaspoons finely chopped garlic
1 teaspoon finely chopped fresh ginger
½ teaspoon ground turmeric
1 teaspoon salt, *or* to taste
500 g (1 lb) potatoes, peeled and cubed
2 cups fresh green peas
2 large tomatoes, chopped
2 teaspoons ground coriander
1 teaspoon toasted ground cummin
1 cup (8 fl oz) hot water

Garnish
2 tablespoons fresh coriander leaves, chopped

Heat ghee and oil mixture in a saucepan and fry onion till soft and golden. Stir in pepper, chillies, garlic, ginger, turmeric and salt. Continue cooking for 2 or 3 minutes then add potatoes and stir till light brown all over.

Add remaining ingredients and hot water, stir well, cover and simmer till vegetables are tender and the oil shows on the surface. Garnish with chopped coriander leaves and serve with chapatis or rice, and accompaniments.

SRI LANKA
YELLOW PUMPKIN CURRY

(Picture on opposite page)

A mild, slightly sweet curry that appeals to children and adults alike. **Charmaine.**

Serves: 6

500 g (1 lb) pumpkin
1 small onion, finely chopped
1 teaspoon finely chopped garlic
3 fresh green chillies, seeded and chopped
8-10 curry leaves
½ teaspoon fenugreek seeds
½ teaspoon ground turmeric
2 teaspoons pounded Maldive fish *or* dried prawns
1½ cups (12 fl oz) thin coconut milk
1 teaspoon salt
½ cup (4 fl oz) thick coconut milk
1 teaspoon black mustard seeds

Peel pumpkin and cut into large chunks. Put into a pan with all the ingredients except the thick coconut milk and mustard seeds. Bring slowly to simmering point and cook gently, uncovered, until pumpkin is almost tender.

Meanwhile, grind the mustard seeds in mortar and pestle and mix with the thick coconut milk. Add to the simmering pot and cook for 5 minutes longer on a very gentle heat.

BURMA

LONG BEANS & TOMATO CURRY

When long beans are not in season, substitute the easily obtained french beans. **Charmaine.**

Serves: 2-3

250 g (8 oz) long beans, chopped 3.75 cm (1½ in)
2 tablespoons peanut oil
6 curry leaves
1 medium onion, finely sliced
1 teaspoon dried shrimp paste
½ teaspoon salt
¼ teaspoon ground black pepper
1 teaspoon chilli powder
1 large tomato, finely chopped
2 teaspoons finely chopped garlic
½ cup hot water
1 teaspoon sesame oil

Heat oil in a saucepan, add curry leaves then add onion and stir till soft and golden. Add dried shrimp paste, salt, pepper, chilli, tomato and garlic. Stir well for 2 minutes, add water, lower heat, cover and simmer till oil comes to the surface.

Raise heat and stir in the beans for 1 minute. Cover and simmer till cooked, crunchy but not mushy. Add sesame oil, stir and serve with rice and accompaniments.

INDIA

FRESH PEANUT CURRY

Serves: 2-4

250 g (½ lb) shelled raw peanuts
½ cup (1½ oz) desiccated coconut
2 teaspoons finely chopped garlic
1 tablespoon ground coriander
½ teaspoon ground turmeric
½ teaspoon ground chilli powder
3 tablespoons oil
2 medium onions, finely sliced
1 tomato, peeled and chopped
1 teaspoon sugar, *or* to taste
1½ teaspoons salt
hot water
½ teaspoon garam masala

Garnish
2 tablespoons chopped fresh coriander leaves

Soak peanuts in water for 2 hours, then boil for 20 minutes. Drain and set aside. Place coconut, garlic, coriander, turmeric and chilli powder in container of electric blender with enough water to allow blades to move freely. Blend to a paste on high speed, remove contents and set aside.

Heat oil and fry onions till soft and golden. Add tomato and the blended mixture and cook, stirring, until it smells fragrant and the oil comes to the surface.

Add nuts, sugar, salt and 1 cup hot water. Bring to the boil, cover and simmer for 15 minutes or until peanuts are cooked. Sprinkle with garam masala and garnish with chopped coriander leaves. Serve with hot rice and accompaniments.

INDIA
POTATO CURRY

(Picture page 91)

For all Irish curry lovers! **Reuben.**

Serves: 3-4

500 g (1 lb) potatoes
1 tablespoon ghee
1 tablespoon oil
½ teaspoon black cummin seeds
½ teaspoon black mustard seeds
1 onion, finely chopped
2 teaspoons finely grated ginger
1 teaspoon ground turmeric
1 teaspoon ground cummin
½ teaspoon chilli powder
1½ teaspoons salt
1 cup (8 fl oz) hot water
1 teaspoon garam masala
2 tablespoons lemon juice

Garnish
2 tablespoons finely chopped fresh mint
  or fresh coriander

Peel potatoes and cut into large cubes. Heat the ghee and oil in a heavy saucepan with a well fitting lid and fry the black cummin and mustard seeds until they pop. Add onion and ginger and fry, stirring, until soft and golden. Add the turmeric, ground cummin and chilli powder, stir quickly, add the salt and the potatoes and toss all together well.

Add hot water to pan, cover and cook on very low heat for 20 minutes. Sprinkle garam masala and lemon juice over, shake pan with lid on, allow to cook for a further 5 to 10 minutes, until potatoes are cooked. Serve garnished with chopped herbs.

INDONESIA
SPICY CABBAGE IN COCONUT MILK

This is called a 'sayur' in Indonesia, and a similar dish is called 'white curry' in Sri Lanka and 'molee' in India. Serve with rice alongside one of the drier types of meat curries. **Charmaine.**

Serves: 4

500 g (1 lb) cabbage
2 onions, chopped
2 cloves garlic
2 fresh red chillies, seeded and chopped,
  or 1 teaspoon chilli powder
1 teaspoon dried shrimp paste
1 daun salam *or* 3 curry leaves
2 tablespoons peanut oil
2 strips lemon rind
1½ cups thick coconut milk
1 teaspoon salt
3 tablespoons tamarind liquid (see Glossary)

Wash and coarsely shred the cabbage. Put chopped onions, garlic, and chillies into container of electric blender and blend to a purée. or grate onions and garlic, and chop chillies finely or substitute chilli powder. wrap the shrimp paste in a piece of foil and roast under the griller for 5 minutes, turning halfway through.

In a wok or large saucepan fry the daun salam or curry leaves in hot oil for 1 minute, turn in the blended mixture and the shrimp paste and fry, stirring, until the mixture turns a darker colour. Stir constantly or mixture might stick to base of pan. Add lemon rind, coconut milk and salt, stir well while bringing to simmering point. Add the cabbage and simmer, uncovered, for a few minutes until the cabbage is cooked but still crisp. Stir in the tamarind liquid and serve.

MUSHROOM & POTATO CURRY

This is the kind of dish that could turn me into a vegetarian. Small new potatoes cut in halves may be used instead of diced large potatoes for a change in appearance and texture. **Charmaine.**

Serves: 4-6

375 g (12 oz) button mushrooms, whole
250 g (8 oz) potatoes, diced
3 tablespoons peanut oil
1 teaspoon dried fenugreek leaves
1 large onion, finely chopped
2 teaspoons finely chopped garlic
1 teaspoon finely chopped fresh ginger
1 large tomato, chopped
2 tablespoons chopped fresh coriander leaves
1 teaspoon chilli powder
1 teaspoon ground turmeric
1 teaspoon salt, *or* to taste
½ cup hot water
½ teaspoon garam masala

Heat oil in a saucepan, add fenugreek leaves, then onion and fry till soft and golden. Stir in garlic, ginger, tomatoes, and coriander leaves and cook, stirring, for 2 minutes. Add chilli powder, turmeric, salt and hot water. Bring to the boil then stir in mushrooms and diced potatoes.

Cover and simmer, stirring occasionally, until potatoes are tender. Sprinkle with garam masala and serve with Indian bread or rice and accompaniments.

VEGETABLE CURRY

Here is the basic white curry. In it you can cook beans, pumpkin, okra, capsicum, potatoes, zucchini, asparagus or other vegetables of your choice. **Charmaine**

Serves: 4-6

3 cups (24 fl oz) thin coconut milk
1 medium onion, finely sliced
2 fresh green chillies seeded and split
½ teaspoon ground turmeric
1 teaspoon finely chopped garlic
½ teaspoon finely grated fresh ginger
5 cm (2 in) cinnamon stick
4 pieces dried daun pandan or rampé leaf
1 stem lemon grass *or* 2 strips lemon rind, optional
8 curry leaves
750 g (1½ lb) vegetables, sliced
salt to taste
1 cup (8 fl oz) thick coconut milk

Put all ingredients, except sliced vegetables, salt and thick coconut milk, in a large saucepan and simmer gently, uncovered, for approximately 10 minutes.

Add sliced vegetables and salt and cook gently until vegetables are just tender. Add thick coconut milk and simmer about 5 minutes longer. Serve with boiled rice, other curries and accompaniments.

CASHEW NUT CURRY

(Picture page 110)

A curry of fresh cashew nuts is one of the delights of Sinhalese cooking. Fresh cashew nuts are not obtainable except in the country in which they are grown, but raw cashews, from health food shops and Chinese grocery stores, make a very good substitute if soaked overnight in cold water. **Charmaine**

Proceed as for vegetable curry (see above), but substitute 250 g (8 oz) raw cashew nuts for sliced vegetables. Simmer for approximately 30 minutes, or until cashews are tender. Serve with boiled rice and other accompaniments.

INDIA
CURRIED DRIED BEANS

Any of the dried beans may be used for this curry. I particularly favour chick peas. **Reuben.**

Serves: 4

250 g (8 oz) dried beans
water
2 teaspoons salt
1½ tablespoons ghee *or* oil
1 large onion, finely chopped
1 teaspoon finely chopped garlic
1 tablespoon finely chopped fresh ginger
1 teaspoon ground turmeric
1 teaspoon garam masala (see page 14)
2 large ripe tomatoes, chopped
1-2 fresh green chillies, seeded and chopped
2 tablespoons chopped fresh mint
2 tablespoons lemon juice

Soak dried beans in plenty of cold water overnight. Drain, rinse and put beans into a large saucepan with water to cover and 1 teaspoon salt. Bring to the boil, cover and cook until tender. Add more hot water during cooking if necessary. Drain and reserve cooking liquid.

Heat ghee in large saucepan and gently fry the onion, garlic and ginger until soft and golden, then add turmeric, garam masala, tomatoes, chillies, mint, remaining teaspoon salt and lemon juice. Add the beans and stir well over medium heat for 5 minutes. Add 1 cup (8 fl oz) reserved liquid, cover and cook over low heat until tomatoes and chillies are soft and the gravy thick. Serve with rice or Indian breads as part of a vegetarian meal.

INDIA
BROWN LENTIL & TOMATO CURRY

Serves: 4

1 cup brown lentils
2 teaspoons ghee
2 tablespoons peanut oil
1 medium onion, thinly sliced
3 tablespoons chopped coriander leaves
2 medium tomatoes, chopped
2 teaspoons finely chopped garlic
1 teaspoon finely chopped fresh ginger
2 teaspoons ground cummin
1 teaspoon chilli powder
1 teaspoon turmeric
salt to taste
1 tablespoon lemon juice
½ teaspoon garam masala

Soak lentils for 2 hours and boil in 4 cups (32 fl oz) water till cooked but still firm. Drain and set aside. Heat ghee and oil and fry onion till soft and golden. Stir in chopped coriander, tomatoes, garlic, ginger and cummin and cook further 3-4 minutes.

Add chilli powder, turmeric, salt and lemon juice and cook till mixture smells aromatic, stirring occasionally. Add lentils, mix thoroughly and cook further 4 minutes. Sprinkle with garam masala and serve with chapatis or rice, and accompaniments.

MALAYSIA
VEGETABLE CURRY

Serves: 6 as an accompaniment

1 onion, finely sliced
½ teaspoon finely chopped garlic
2 fresh red *or* green chillies, seeded and sliced
½ teaspoon dried shrimp paste
½ teaspoon ground turmeric
1 cup (8 fl oz) thin coconut milk
1 large potato, peeled and diced
3 cups coarsely shredded cabbage
1 teaspoon salt
1 cup (8 fl oz) thick coconut milk
lemon juice to taste

Put the onion, garlic, chillies, dried shrimp paste, turmeric and thin coconut milk into a saucepan and bring to simmering point. Add potato and cook for 10 minutes or until potato is half cooked.

Add cabbage and salt, cook for 3 minutes, then add the thick coconut milk and stir gently until cabbage is cooked. Remove from heat and add lemon juice to taste.

MOGHUL VEGETABLE CURRY

I argued that Reuben was being heavy-handed with the spices but when I tasted the result I had to admit he had a winner. **Charmaine.**

Serves: 4

4 cups diced mixed vegetables (carrots, potatoes, beans, peas)
¼ cup (3 oz) blanched almonds
6 cloves
2 teaspoons cardamom seeds
1 teaspoon dried fenugreek leaves
5 cm (2 in) cinnamon stick, broken
2 teaspoons chopped garlic
½ teaspoon chilli powder
½ teaspoon ground turmeric
hot water
3 tablespoons ghee
1 large onion, finely sliced
¼ teaspoon ground saffron
½ cup (4 fl oz) natural yoghurt
salt to taste
½ cup (4 fl oz) water

Place almonds, cloves, cardamom, fenugreek leaves, cinnamon, garlic, chilli powder and turmeric in container of electric blender with enough hot water to enable blades to move freely. Blend to a paste on high speed, remove contents and set aside.

Heat ghee in a saucepan and fry onion till soft and golden. Stir in the paste and fry till it smells fragrant and ghee comes to the surface. Add saffron powder and stir in mixed vegetables and yoghurt. Add salt and water and bring to the boil, cover and simmer till vegetables are tender. Serve with Indian bread and accompaniments.

SPINACH AND CHEESE CURRY

This is Reuben's speciality. He simply loves the flavour of fenugreek leaves and if I don't watch him he will put them in just about everything. **Charmaine.**

Serves: 2-4

1 bunch spinach, leaves only
250 g (8 oz) ricotta cheese, cubed
oil for frying
2 teaspoons dried fenugreek leaves
1 large onion, finely sliced
2 teaspoons finely chopped garlic
1 teaspoon finely chopped fresh ginger
2 teaspoons ground cummin
½ teaspoon ground turmeric
1 medium tomato, chopped
1 teaspoon salt
juice of half lemon

Boil spinach in 1 cup (8 fl oz) water for 5 minutes, drain, chop and set aside. Fry cheese cubes to a golden brown and set aside.

Heat 3 tablespoons oil in a saucepan, stir in fenugreek leaves then onion and fry till soft and golden. Stir in garlic, ginger, cummin, turmeric, tomato, salt and lemon juice. Cook till oil comes to the surface and the mixture smells fragrant.

Mix in the spinach and cook for a further 5 minutes. Gently stir in the cheese cubes, heat through and serve with rice and accompaniments.

BURMA

PUMPKIN & COCONUT CURRY

This is a soupy curry and is quite a favourite in Burma. **Reuben.**

Serves: 2-4

500 g (1 lb) pumpkin, peeled and cubed
1 large onion, finely sliced
2 teaspoons finely chopped garlic
1 teaspoon turmeric
1 teaspoon chilli powder
1 teaspoon salt
½ teaspoon ground black pepper
1 teaspoon dried shrimp paste
2 tablespoons creamed coconut *or*
    ½ cup thick coconut milk
1½ cups (12 fl oz) hot water
2 fresh green chillies, sliced

Place all ingredients, except pumpkin, into a saucepan and bring to the boil. Lower heat and simmer for 5 minutes. Then add pumpkin, cover and simmer until tender. Serve with boiled rice and accompaniments.

INDIA

LENTIL PUREE

(Picture page 91)

A staple dish throughout India. For a fine flavoured garnish, fry 2 large onions, finely sliced, until brown, and scatter on top of the dhal. **Charmaine.**

Serves: 4-5

250 g (8 oz) red lentils
2 tablespoons ghee *or* oil
1 onion, finely sliced
2 cloves garlic, sliced
1 teaspoon finely chopped fresh ginger
½ teaspoon ground turmeric
3 cups (24 fl oz) hot water
1 teaspoon salt, *or* to taste
½ teaspoon garam masala, optional

Wash lentils, discarding those that float. Drain well. In a saucepan heat ghee or oil and fry onion, garlic and ginger until golden brown. Add turmeric and stir for a few seconds, then add the drained lentils and fry for a minute. Add hot water and bring to the boil, reduce heat, cover and simmer until lentils are soft before adding salt and garam masala. Continue cooking until the consistency of porridge.

INDIA

BENGAL EGGPLANT CURRY

The mustard oil imparts quite a distinctive flavour, but if you cannot buy it easily substitute peanut oil. **Reuben.**

Serves: 4

2 tablespoons each of mustard oil and peanut oil
1 teaspoon mustard seeds
1 teaspoon fenugreek seeds
½ teaspoon fennel seeds
1 large onion, finely sliced
1 large eggplant, cubed
1 teaspoon finely chopped garlic
2 teaspoons ground coriander
1 teaspoon ground cummin
1 teaspoon chilli powder
2 whole bay leaves
½ teaspoon turmeric
1 cup fresh green peas
1 teaspoon salt, *or* to taste
1 tablespoon vinegar
1 cup hot water

Heat oils in a saucepan and fry mustard, fenugreek and fennel seeds till mustard seeds start to pop, then add onion and fry till soft and golden. Stir in the cubed eggplant and continue to fry a further 5 minutes.

Add the rest of the ingredients and stir well for 2 more minutes. Stir in hot water, bring to the boil, cover and simmer till vegetables are cooked but not mushy. Serve with hot rice and accompaniments.

accompaníme

In any curry meal, it is those titillating morsels like chutneys, pickles, pappadams, sambals and so on that complement the main dishes, providing accents of flavour and texture which make a good curry meal so memorable. The creative cook will allow imagination free rein this area, adding to the menu accompaniments which give a stamp of individuality.

While most of the recipes for accompaniments may be served with the main dishes of another country's cuisine, it appears that the strong garlic and prawn flavours of some Burmese and Thai accompaniments are only at home with Burmese and Thai foods. They may even be served with some Malaysian or Indonesian dishes, but are completely at variance with Indian flavours. So while you can mix and match main dishes of one country with sambals and salads from another, be discriminating enough to keep strong flavours from dominating a gently spiced meal.

s

THAILAND
CHILLI SALAD

10 fresh green chillies, chopped
1 tablespoon prawn powder
2 teaspoons grated garlic
1-2 tablespoons fish sauce
3 teaspoons finely chopped lemon rind
juice of half a lemon

Mix all ingredients together and serve with curry and boiled rice.

INDIA
FRESH MINT CHUTNEY

In addition to its refreshing flavour this chutney has a pretty green colour and brightens any table. **Charmaine.**

1 cup (4 oz) firmly packed mint leaves
6 spring onions, including green leaves
2 fresh green chillies, roughly chopped
½ teaspoon chopped garlic, optional
1 teaspoon salt
2 teaspoons sugar
1 teaspoon garam masala (see page 14)
⅓ cup lemon juice
2 tablespoons water

In the absence of the grinding stones used in India for reducing grains to flour, and others which make 'wet' masalas and fresh chutneys, a powerful electric blender is the Western cook's best friend when preparing Indian food.

Put mint into blender together with onions cut into short lengths and all other ingredients. Blend on high speed to a smooth purée. If blender is not available finely chop mint, onions and chillies and pound a little at a time in mortar and pestle. Then mix in remaining ingredients.

Pack the chutney into a small dish, smooth the surface, cover and chill. Serve as an accompaniment with rice and curries, chapatis, thosai and other savoury snacks.

INDONESIA
BASIC SAMBAL SEASONING

A quick, convenient method to present the myriad dishes that comprise an Indonesian meal. If you like hot food you will find it useful to make up a quantity of this base, which you can cook and keep bottled in the refrigerator ready to add to such varied ingredients as boiled or fried potatoes, breadfruit, yams or other starchy vegetables; hard-boiled eggs; bean curd cut in dice or strips and fried; fresh or dried fish, fried; fried prawns and other shell fish; crisp-fried strips of meat or liver. There is no end to the variations on this theme. **Charmaine.**

15-20 large dried chillies
3 large onions, roughly chopped
8 cloves garlic
2 teaspoons dried shrimp paste
½ cup peanut oil, *or* more as required
1 cup (8 fl oz) tamarind liquid
3 teaspoons salt
2 tablespoons palm sugar *or* substitute

Soak chillies in hot water for 20 minutes. In container of electric blender grind the soaked chillies, onions, garlic and shrimp paste, with enough oil to help the blades draw down the solid ingredients: it may be necessary to use more than half the oil, depending on the size and shape of the blender. When blended to a smooth paste, heat remaining oil in a wok or frying pan and when hot put in the blended ingredients. Fry over medium heat, stirring constantly, until mixture is cooked and dark in colour and oil separates and shows around edges. Wash out blender container with the tamarind liquid, add to pan with salt and sugar and simmer for a few minutes longer, stirring. Cool completely and bottle. Store in refrigerator. (If mixture has been cooked in a wok, turn it into a glass or earthenware bowl to cool.)

To use: Heat the required amount (in the proportions of approximately 1 tablespoon to 250 g or 8 oz of the main ingredient) and stir-fry the already-cooked main ingredient in it briefly. If a gravy is required, add ½-1 cup (4-8 fl oz) thick coconut milk and heat to simmering point, stirring constantly.

INDIA
SPICED SPINACH

This recipe turns this bland vegetable into an extremely tasty dish. **Reuben.**

Serves: 4

500 g (1 lb) spinach
2 teaspoons toasted cummin seeds, crushed
1 clove garlic crushed with
 ½ teaspoon salt
1 teaspoon finely chopped fresh ginger
1 green chilli, finely chopped
salt to taste
½ teaspoon garam marsala
1 cup (8 fl oz) natural yoghurt

Wash spinach well, place in a saucepan with ½ cup water, cover and cook for 10 minutes. Drain and place spinach in container of electric blender and purée at high speed. Remove, drain and set aside. Toast cummin seeds in a dry pan till brown and fragrant, set aside.

Add garlic, ginger, chilli, salt, and garam masala to yoghurt and mix well. Place spinach on serving dish, spread over with yoghurt mixture and sprinkle with crushed cummin. Serve with boiled rice and curry.

SRI LANKA
CUCUMBER SAMBOL

(Picture page 110)

I have fond memories of this sambol from my Sri Lankan background. Reuben likes it with very thin slices of raw bitter gourd, which is a Burmese version. **Charmaine.**

1 large *or* 2 small green cucumbers
2 teaspoons salt
½ cup (4 fl oz) thick coconut milk
1 fresh red chilli, seeded and sliced
1 fresh green chilli, seeded and sliced
1 small onion, cut in paper-thin slices
2 tablespoons lemon juice

Peel cucumber and slice very thinly. Put in a bowl, sprinkle with salt and let stand for at least 30 minutes. Press out all liquid and if too salty, rinse with cold water. Drain well.

Mix with remaining ingredients and serve as an accompaniment to a curry meal.

INDONESIA
FRIED CHILLI SAMBAL

Cooled, then stored in an airtight bottle, this sambal will keep for weeks in the refrigerator. When serving, use a teaspoon for portions and warn guests it should be eaten in tiny quantities with rice, not by itself: this torrid sambal is an acquired taste. However, it is enjoyed on crisp crackers, in sandwiches, on steaks — in fact there is no limit to the ways a sambal addict will use it. **Charmaine.**

Yield: about 1 cup

6 large fresh red chillies, roughly chopped
1 large onion
6 cloves garlic
3 tablespoons peanut oil
8 candle nuts or 5 Brazil nuts, finely grated
½ teaspoon laos powder
1 tablespoon dried shrimp paste
1 teaspoon salt
5 tablespoons tamarind liquid
2 tablespoons palm sugar *or* substitute

Put chillies, onion and garlic in container of electric blender and blend to a pulp. If blender is small, blend in small portions. It might be necessary to stop and start the motor several times to draw the onions and chillies down on to the blades. When everything has been blended smoothly, heat the oil in a small frying pan or a saucepan and fry the blended mixture over low heat, stirring, for 5 minutes or until well cooked but not brown. Add candle nuts, laos, dried shrimp paste and salt. Crush the shrimp paste against the side of the pan and fry, stirring, until mixture is well blended.

Add tamarind liquid and sugar, stir and simmer until well fried and reddish-brown in colour and the oil separates from the mixture. Cool. This sambal is not served hot from the fire.

Note: If electric blender is not available, seed the chillies and chop very finely. Peel and chop onion finely, crush garlic with salt, then proceed as above.

Fried Chilli Sambal (Sambal Bajak) and Sambal Ulek (see Glossary) may be purchased ready-made in some shops selling Asian ingredients.

INDIA
ONION & TOMATO SAMBAL

The sweet-sour flavours of tamarind and sugar raise this above the ordinary run-of-the-mill class of sambals. **Charmaine.**

Serves: 6

2 medium onions
salt
1 tablespoon tamarind pulp *or*
    1 teaspoon instant tamarind
¼ cup hot water
2 tablespoons brown sugar *or* jaggery
2 firm ripe tomatoes
1 tablespoon finely shredded fresh ginger
2 *or* 3 fresh red *or*
    green chillies, seeded and sliced
2 tablespoons chopped fresh coriander

Peel the onions, cut them in halves lengthways and then cut across into fine slices. Sprinkle generously with salt and leave for an hour. Press out all the liquid and rinse once in cold water. Drain well.

Soak tamarind pulp in hot water for a few minutes, then squeeze to dissolve pulp and strain, discarding the seeds. If using instant tamarind, dissolve in the hot water. Dissolve brown sugar in the tamarind liquid

Scald tomatoes, peel and dice. Combine all the ingredients, add salt to taste, chill and serve. Salads of this type are served as accompaniments to rice and curries.

SRI LANKA
RED COCONUT SAMBOL

(Picture page 109)

This is one of Reuben's favourite sambols. He prefers it with ½ teaspoon crushed garlic added to the recipe, but whether you follow his idea or not depends on your level of garlic tolerance and that of your close associates! **Charmaine.**

Serves: 6-8

1 cup (3 oz) desiccated coconut
1 teaspoon salt
1-2 teaspoons chilli powder, to taste
2 teaspoons paprika (for colour)
2 teaspoons Maldive fish *or* prawn powder, optional
3 tablespoons lemon juice
1 small onion, finely chopped
2 fresh red *or* green chillies, seeded and chopped

Combine all the ingredients in a bowl and mix with the hands, so that the coconut is moistened by the onion and lemon juice. If necessary sprinkle a couple of tablespoons of hot water over so that the coconut is thoroughly moistened.

INDIA
BANANA RAITA

(Picture page 109)

Serves: 6

3 large ripe bananas
lemon juice
1 cup (8 fl oz) natural yoghurt
3 tablespoons freshly grated *or* desiccated coconut
½ teaspoon salt
2 teaspoons sugar
½ teaspoon ground toasted cummin seeds

Slice the bananas and sprinkle with lemon juice. Combine the yoghurt with the other ingredients. If desiccated coconut is used, moisten it first by sprinkling with about 2 tablespoons water and tossing it with the fingers until it is no longer dry. Chill and serve.

BURMA

POUNDED PRAWN PASTE

I must warn readers that it takes someone born or brought up in Burma to fully appreciate this pungent paste. **Charmaine.**

To be eaten in very small quantities with rice.

2 tablespoons prawn powder
2 tablespoons dried shrimp paste
2 medium onions
4 cloves garlic
2 teaspoons chilli powder, optional
1 teaspoon salt
juice of half a lemon

Press the dried shrimp paste into a flat cake, wrap in foil and put under a hot griller for 15 minutes, turning to cook both sides. Wrap onions and garlic in foil and put under griller with the dried shrimp paste. Pound together these ingredients in a mortar and pestle. Then mix in remaining ingredients.

Alternatively, the crumbled dried shrimp paste, peeled onions and garlic can be blended in an electric blender with lemon juice and combined with other ingredients.

SRI LANKA

GROUND ONION & CHILLI SAMBOL

This simple sambol is as basic to the food of Sri Lanka as salt and pepper are to Western food. Very hot, very acid and distinctly salty, it is often the only accompaniment to serve with rice, boiled yams, manioc or sweet potato, or any of the starches that are the staple of the native diet. **Charmaine**

10 dried chillies
1 tablespoon pounded Maldive fish or
    dried prawns
1 small onion, chopped
lemon juice and salt to taste

Remove stalks from chillies. If a less hot result is preferred, shake out the seeds. Pound all the ingredients together in a mortar and pestle. In Sri Lanka this would be either pounded or ground on the grinding stone. (It can be done in a blender, but a wet result is not desirable, since the end result should be a paste.)

Serve with rice.

MALAYSIA

BEEF SAMBAL

When we were served this in Kuala Lumpur, fresh laos was used, and the garlic stepped up. Very interesting indeed. **Reuben**

Serves: 4

250 g (8 oz) scotch fillet, sliced thin
2 tablespoons peanut oil
5 candle nuts or 4 Brazil kernels, chopped
1 teaspoon dried shrimp paste
2 medium onions, roughly chopped
5 dried red chillies
½ teaspoon ground turmeric
1 teaspoon ground laos
1 teaspoon chopped garlic
1 teaspoon tamarind paste
1 teaspoon salt
2 teaspoons sugar

Slice beef into thin shreds. Blend all ingredients except oil to a fine paste in an electric blender, adding a little hot water to facilitate blending.

Heat oil in saucepan or wok. Add mixture to hot oil and stir-fry till mixture smells cooked and oil surfaces. Add sliced beef and stir till well coated with the mixture. Cover and simmer till gravy thickens (about 5 minutes). Serve with boiled rice and curry.

MALAYSIA
OMELETTE SAMBAL

Serves: 4-6

4 eggs, slightly beaten
3 tablespoons peanut oil
1 large onion, finely sliced
2 red chillies
1 teaspoon dried shrimp paste
1 teaspoon garlic chopped
½ teaspoon ground black pepper
salt to taste

Heat oil in a wok or saucepan. Fry onion till soft and golden. Blend chillies, dried shrimp paste, garlic, pepper and salt to a paste in an electric blender, adding a little water to facilitate blending. Add spice mixture to onions and stir-fry till mixture smells fragrant, and oil comes to the surface. Stir in beaten eggs and cook into one large omelette. Divide into 4-6 segments and serve with rice and curry.

INDONESIA
PIQUANT FRIED PRAWN SAMBAL

Serves: 6

500 g (1 lb) shelled raw prawns
2 tablespoons peanut oil
1 onion, finely chopped
1½ teaspoons finely chopped garlic
½ teaspoon finely grated fresh ginger
2 teaspoons sambal ulek *or* 4 fresh red chillies
½ teaspoon laos powder
2 strips thinly peeled lemon rind, chopped
⅓ cup tamarind liquid
1 teaspoon salt
1 teaspoon palm sugar *or* substitute

If prawns are large, chop prawns into pieces the size of a peanut. Small shrimp or school prawns may be used whole. Heat oil in a frying pan and fry onion, garlic and ginger until onion is soft and starts to turn golden. Add sambal ulek, laos powder and lemon rind, then add chopped prawns and fry, stirring constantly, until prawns change colour.

Add tamarind liquid and simmer on low heat until gravy is thick and oil starts to separate. Stir in salt and sugar. Taste and correct seasoning if necessary. Serve as a side dish with rice and curries.

MALAYSIA
SAMBAL UDANG

Serves: 6

750 g (1½ lb) medium-sized prawns, shelled and de-veined
2 tablespoons peanut oil
6 dried red chillies
1 medium onion, roughly chopped
6 candle nuts, *or* 4 Brazil kernels, chopped
1 teaspoon dried shrimp paste
2 teaspoons chopped garlic
1 teaspoon chopped fresh ginger
2 teaspoons tamarind paste
1 teaspoon salt
2 teaspoons sugar

Place chillies, onion, kernels, dried shrimp paste, garlic, ginger and tamarind paste in container of electric blender. Add a little water to assist movement of the blades, and blend to a smooth paste.

Heat wok or saucepan, add oil and when hot add blended mixture. Stir-fry for a few minutes till mixture smells cooked and oil comes to the surface. Add prawns and stir-fry till well coated with the mixture then add salt and sugar. Continue to stir-fry till prawns are cooked and gravy thickens. Serve with rice and curry.

THAILAND
FRESH LEMON GRASS SALAD

4 stems lemon grass
5 fresh red chillies, chopped
1-2 tablespoons fish sauce

Use only the pale, tender base of the lemon grass. Wash well and chop finely. Place in a bowl, add chillies and fish sauce. Mix well and serve with curry and boiled rice.

THAILAND
BRAISED BITTER MELON SALAD

2 x 7.5 cm (3 in) tender bitter melon
1 tablespoon peanut oil
2 teaspoons grated garlic
4 fresh red chillies, chopped
1 tablespoon prawn powder
1-2 tablespoons fish sauce
½ teaspoon ground black pepper

Cut bitter melon lengthwise in half. Slice thinly across and set aside. Heat wok, add oil and when hot, stir-fry the bitter melon for 1 minute, then stir in the garlic and red chillies for another minute. Add the rest of the ingredients. Stir and cover for 1 more minute, then remove to a dish. Serve with curry and boiled rice.

BURMA
SHRIMP PASTE SAUTE

I first tried this in Mandalay and have been hooked on it ever since. **Reuben.**

½ cup (4 fl oz) vegetable oil
1 onion, chopped
3 teaspoons finely chopped garlic
¼ teaspoon turmeric
1 tablespoon dried shrimp paste
3-4 tomatoes, quartered
1 cup (3 oz) dried prawn powder
2 green chillies, sliced
1 tablespoon tamarind liquid
½ teaspoon salt *or* to taste

Heat oil until very hot, reduce heat to medium and fry onion, garlic and turmeric till dark golden and nearly sticking to pan. Add dried shrimp paste, tomatoes, prawn powder, green chillies and tamarind liquid. Stir and cook until all the liquid has evaporated and oil separates from the mass. Add salt to taste.

SRI LANKA
PRAWN BLACHAN

In Colombo, fresh coconut is used and the ingredients ground on a stone. It is one of the 'special occasion' accompaniments. **Charmaine.**

1 cup dried prawn powder
½ cup (1½ oz) desiccated coconut
2 teaspoons chilli powder *or* to taste
2 medium onions, chopped
5 cloves garlic, sliced
1 tablespoon finely chopped fresh ginger
⅔ cup lemon juice
1 teaspoon salt, *or* to taste

Put prawn powder in a dry frying pan and heat for a few minutes, stirring. Turn on to a large plate. Put desiccated coconut in the same pan and heat, stirring, until a rich brown colour. Turn on to a plate to cool.

Put other ingredients except prawn powder into blender container, cover and blend until smooth. Add prawn powder and desiccated coconut, cover and blend again, adding a little water if necessary to bind ingredients. Scrape down sides of container occasionally with a spatula. Turn on to a plate and shape into a round, flat cake. Serve with rice and curries.

INDIA
BOMBAY DUCK

A pungent dried fish which is served as an accompaniment to rice and curry meals. Sold in packets, they should be cut into pieces about 5 cm (2 in) in length and deep fried in hot oil until light golden brown. Drain and serve as a crisp nibble between mouthfuls of rice.

An alternative method is to fry finely sliced onions in the same oil after the Bombay ducks are fried, and if liked, some broken dried chillies may be fried along with the onions. Fry slowly, stirring, until onions are golden brown. Add a little salt and sugar, stir well, combine with the fried Bombay duck and serve as a sambal.

INDIA
BEETROOT RAITA

(Picture on opposite page)

Charmaine's recipe below is a classic. Sprinkle it with a teaspoon of lightly toasted ground cummin to see what happens. **Reuben.**

Serves: 4

1 cup (5 oz) canned beetroot
1 cup (8 fl oz) natural yoghurt
salt to taste

Chop the beetroot roughly and mix into the yoghurt, adding a little of the juice from the can to give colour and flavour. Taste and add more salt if desired. Chill and serve cold as a cooling accompaniment to a curry meal.

INDIA
FRESH CORIANDER & COCONUT CHUTNEY

(Picture on opposite page)

Anything with fresh coriander and garlic in it pleases Reuben immensely. He has converted photographer, Reg Morrison. Whenever he comes to dine with us, Reuben whips up a batch of this chutney. **Charmaine.**

Serves: 6

1 cup (8 oz) fresh coriander herb
2 tablespoons desiccated coconut
3 tablespoons water
1 teaspoon chopped garlic
1 green chilli, seeded
1 teaspoon garam masala
1 teaspoon salt
2 tablespoons lemon juice

Put the well-washed coriander into container of electric blender with all other ingredients and blend on high speed until smooth. If necessary, add a little water to facilitate blending, but do not make the mixture too wet.

BURMA
DRY BALACHAUNG

(Picture on opposite page, and on page 56)

Brings back memories of Burma. In an orthodox Jewish home we substituted Mergui salt fish for the prawns. Even great as a sandwich filling. **Reuben.**

20 cloves garlic
4 medium onions, finely sliced
2 cups (16 fl oz) peanut oil
1 x 250 g (8 oz) packet of prawn powder
 teaspoons chilli powder, optional
2 teaspoons salt
1 teaspoon dried shrimp paste
½ cup (4 fl oz) vinegar

Peel garlic, cut into thin slices. Cut onions into thin slices. Heat oil and fry onion and garlic separately on low heat until golden. Lift out immediately and set aside. They will become crisp and darken as they cool.
    Pour off all but 1 cup oil and in this, fry prawn powder for 5 minutes. Add chilli powder, salt and shrimp paste mixed with vinegar, stir well and fry until crisp. Allow to cool completely. Mix in fried onion and garlic, stirring to distribute evenly. Store in an airtight jar. Serve with rice or noodles, and Burmese curries.

INDIA
TOMATO & SPRING ONION SAMBAL

(Picture on opposite page)

Try this sprinkled over with ½ teaspoon garam masala. **Reuben.**

I don't agree. I like it just the way it is. **Charmaine.**

Serves: 4

2 large firm red tomatoes
½ cup (2 oz) finely chopped spring onions,
    green leaves and all
½ teaspoon chilli powder
½ teaspoons salt *or* to taste
2-3 tablespoons lemon juice

Cut the tomatoes in small dice and sprinkle with all the other ingredients, tossing gently until well mixed. Cover and chill until required and serve as an accompaniment to rice and curry.

Accompaniments to a curry meal. Tomato and Spring Onion Sambal; Beetroot Raita; Fresh Coriander and Coconut Chutney; Dry Balachaung; all these recipes on opposite page; Red Coconut Sambol, recipe page 104; grilled Pappadams, recipe on page 111; Banana Raita, recipe page 104.

From front: Beef Curry, recipe page 34; Fried Eggplant Sambol; Pappadams; Coconut Sambol; all these recipes on opposite page; Cucumber Sambol, recipe page 103, Cashew Nut Curry, recipe page 96; Yellow Rice, recipe page 25.

INDIA
COCONUT CHUTNEY

(Picture page 91)

Asafoetida! That's Reuben's touch. Try it as directed for a new dimension in taste. **Charmaine.**

Serves: 6-8

Half a coconut, freshly grated *or*
   1 cup (3 oz) desiccated coconut
1 lemon *or* lime
2 *or* 3 fresh green chillies
½ cup (¾ oz) chopped fresh mint
1 teaspoon salt
2 teaspoons ghee *or* oil
⅛ teaspoon ground asafoetida, optional
1 teaspoon black mustard seeds
1 teaspoon black cummin seeds
10 curry leaves
½ teaspoon urad dhal

If using desiccated coconut, sprinkle with about ¼ cup (2 fl oz) water and toss to moisten evenly. Peel the lemon or lime so that no white pith remains. Cut in pieces and remove the seeds. Put lemon into container of electric blender with the seeded and roughly chopped chillies and mint and blend until smooth. Add the coconut and continue blending to a smooth paste, scraping down sides of blender and adding a little more liquid if necessary. Add the salt and mix.

Heat ghee or oil in a small pan and fry the remaining ingredients, stirring frequently, until mustard seeds pop and dhal is golden. Mix with the coconut, pat into a flat cake and serve as an accompaniment to a curry meal.

PAPPADAMS

(Picture on opposite page)

Allow 2 per person

pappadams
peanut oil for deep frying

These spicy lentil wafers are sold dried in packets. Heat the oil and test with a small piece of pappadam: if the oil is not hot enough the piece will sink to the bottom and stay there. The oil should be hot enough for the pappadam to double its size within the first two or three seconds.

Deep fry one pappadam at a time for three or four seconds in the oil. They will swell and turn pale golden. Drain well on absorbent paper. Pappadams are best fried just before serving, but they may be cooled and stored in an air-tight container if prepared a few hours beforehand.

SRI LANKA
FRIED EGGPLANT SAMBOL

(Picture on opposite page)

2 eggplants
2 teaspoons salt
2 teaspoons ground turmeric
oil for frying
3 fresh red *or* green chillies
2 small onions
lemon juice
3 tablespoons thick coconut milk

Slice eggplants thinly, rub with salt and turmeric, put in a bowl and leave at least 1 hour. Drain off liquid and dry eggplant on paper towels.

Fry in hot oil and drain on absorbent paper. Mix with seeded and chopped chillies, finely sliced onion, lemon juice to taste and 3 tablespoons thick coconut milk.

SRI LANKA
ROASTED COCONUT SAMBOL

In Sri Lanka, this is a very popular accompaniment to a meal of rice and curries. The fresh coconut is halved, roasted in the ashes of a fire until dark brown, then ground on a stone. This is the easy method that I had to learn when deprived of a constant supply of fresh coconuts and household help to grind them! **Charmaine.**

1 cup (3 oz) desiccated coconut
2 medium onions, finely chopped
1 teaspoon salt
2 teaspoons maldive fish or dried prawn powder
4 tablespoons lemon juice *or* to taste

In a heavy based frying pan heat the coconut, stirring constantly so it will brown evenly. It should be a deep brown, not merely golden, so that it gives this sambol its distinctive flavour. Remove from pan immediately and spread on a plate to cool. Combine all ingredients in electric blender, cover and blend until a smooth paste is formed. If liquid is insufficient it may be necessary to add a little more lemon juice or finely grated onion. Shape the paste into a flat cake on a small plate. Mark the top in a criss-cross pattern with the back of a knife.

MALAYSIA
MALAY VEGETABLE PICKLES

1 cup (2½ oz) carrot sticks
1 cup (2½ oz) green beans
10 fresh red and green chillies
1 green cucumber
half a small cauliflower
2 tablespoons peanut oil
1 teaspoon finely chopped garlic
2 teaspoons finely grated fresh ginger
3 candlenuts *or* Brazil kernels, grated
1 teaspoon ground turmeric
½ cup (4 fl oz) white vinegar
½ cup (4 fl oz) water
2 teaspoons sugar
1 teaspoon salt

Cut carrots into julienne strips. Cut beans into pieces of the same length, then slice each piece in two lengthways. If beans are very young and slender it will not be necessary to slice them. Leave the chillies whole, but remove stems. Peel cucumber and cut in half lengthways, remove seeds and slice into pieces the same size as the carrots and beans. Cut cauliflowers into sprigs, leaving a bit of stem on each piece.

Heat oil in a saucepan and fry garlic and ginger on low heat for 1 minute, stirring. Add grated nuts and turmeric and stir for a few seconds longer. Add vinegar, water, sugar and salt and bring to the boil. Add carrots and beans, chillies and cauliflower sprigs, return to the boil and boil for 3 minutes. Add cucumber and boil for 1 minute longer.

Remove immediately to an earthenware or glass bowl and allow to cool. Use at once or bottle and store in refrigerator for a week or two.

GLOSSARY

AJOWAN
Bot.: *Carum ajowan*
Fam.: *Umbelliferae*
Hindi: *ajwain*

Of the same family as parsley and cummin, the seeds look like parsley or celery seeds, but have the flavour of thyme. It is used in Indian cooking, particularly in lentil dishes that provide the protein in vegetarian diets, both as a flavouring and as a carminative. It is one of the seeds used to flavour the crisp-fried snacks made from lentil flour. *Ajwain* water is used as a medicine in stomach ailments.

AMCHUR

Dried green mango, usually available in powder form. Used as an acid flavouring ingredient in Indian cooking.

AROMATIC GINGER

see galangal, lesser

ASAFOETIDA
Bot: *Ferula asafoetida*
Fam.: *Umbelliferae*
Hindi: *hing*
Tamil: *perunkaya*
Burmese: *sheingho*

Used in minute quantities in Indian cooking, its main purpose is to prevent flatulence. It is obtained from the resinous gum of a plant growing in Afghanistan and Iran. The stalks are cut close to the root and the milky fluid that flows out is dried into the resin sold as *asafoetida*. Although it has quite an unpleasant smell by itself, a tiny piece the size of a pea attached to the inside of the lid of a cooking pot adds a certain flavour that is much prized, apart from its medicinal properties.

ATTA

Fine wholemeal flour used in making Indian flat breads. Substitute fine wholemeal sold in health food stores. *Atta* flour can be bought from stores specialising in Asian foods.

BAMBOO SHOOT
Malay: *rebong*
Indonesian: *rebung*

Sold in cans, either water-packed or braised. Unless otherwise stated, the recipes in this book use the water-packed variety. After opening can, store in a bowl of fresh water in the refrigerator, changing water daily, for up to 10 days. Winter bamboo shoots are much smaller and more tender, and are called for in certain recipes; however, if they are not available, use the larger variety.

BASIL (SWEET BASIL)
Bot.: *Ocimum basilicum*
Fam.: *Labitae*
Hindi: *babuitulsi*
Thai: *horapa*
Malay: *selaseb, kemangi*
Indonesian: *kemangi*

Used in Indonesian cooking, the leaves add distinctive flavour to those dishes requiring it.

BAY
Bot.: *Laurus nobilis*
Fam.: *Lauraceae*

Almost universally used in European cooking. There is a rather similar leaf, known as *tejpattar*, used in Indian cooking.

BEAN SPROUTS

Green *mung* beans are normally used for bean sprouts. They are sold fresh in most Chinese stores and in certain supermarkets and health food stores. The canned variety is not recommended. Substitute thinly sliced celery for a similar texture but different flavour. Fresh bean sprouts can be stored in a refrigerator for a week in a plastic bag; alternatively, cover with water and change water daily.

BESAN (CHICK PEA FLOUR)

Available in most stores selling Asian foods. Pea flour from health food stores can be substituted, but if it is coarse pass it through a fine sieve before using. Alternatively, roast yellow split peas in a heavy pan, stirring constantly and taking care not to burn them. Cool. then blend at high speed in an electric blender or pound with a mortar and pestle. Sift, then store the fine flour in an airtight container. *Besan* has a distinctive taste, and ordinary wheat flour cannot be substituted.

BITTER MELON (BALSAM PEAR)

Belonging to the squash family, this vegetable can best be described as looking like a cucumber with lumps. Its bitterness is due to the high quinine content. During the season it may be obtained fresh from Chinese grocers, or canned, from Asian specialty stores. As a fresh vegetable, its refrigerator life is 10-12 days. It may be used in stir-fries with meats or alone as a vegetable dish.

BLACHAN

The commercial spelling of *blacan*. See dried shrimp paste.

BOMBAY DUCK

Not a bird, despite its name, this is a variety of fish that is salted and dried. It is sold in packets and should be cut into pieces no more than 2.5 cm (1 inch) long. Deep fried or grilled, it is served as an accompaniment to a meal of rice and curry, and should be nibbled in little pieces.

CANDLE NUT
Bot.: *Aleurites moluccana*
Fam.: *Euphorbiaceae*
Malay: *buah keras*
Indonesian: *kemiri*

A hard oily nut used to flavour and thicken Indonesian and Malaysian curries. The name arises because the nuts, when threaded on the mid-rib of a palm leaf, are used as a primitive candle. Use Brazil kernels as a substitute, though their flavour is sweeter than that of the candle nut.

CARDAMOM
Bot.: *Elettaria cardamomum*
Fam.: *Zingiberaceae*
Hindi: *illaichi*
Sinhalese: *enasal*
Burmese: *phalazee*
Thai: *kravan*
Malay: *buah pelaga*
Indonesian: *kapulaga*

Next to saffron, the world's most expensive spice. Cardamoms grow mainly in India and Ceylon, and are the seed pods of a member of the ginger family. The dried seed pods are either pale green or brown, according to variety. Sometimes they are bleached white. They are added, either whole or bruised, to pilaus and other rice dishes, spiced curries and other preparations or sweets. When ground cardamom is called for, the seed pods are opened and discarded and only the small black or brown seeds are ground. For full flavour, it is best to grind them just before using. There is one brand of 'ground decorticated cardamom' that seems to preserve extremely well the essential oils and fragrances of this exotic spice, but if you cannot buy a really good ground cardamom, crush the seeds in a mortar as required.

CASHEW NUT (CASHEWS)
Hindi: *kaju*
Malay: *gaju*
Sinhalese: *cadju*

A sweet, kidney-shaped nut. In countries where the cashew tree is not grown, it is not possible to get the milky sweet fresh cashews. However, it is possible to buy raw cashews (as distinct from the roasted and salted cashews sold as snacks); nut shops, health food stores and grocers specialising in Asian ingredients stock the raw cashews.

CELLOPHANE NOODLES or BEAN THREAD VERMICELLI
Thai: *woon sen*
Malay: *sohoon, tunghoon*
Indonesian: *sotanghoon*

Fine, transparent noodles made from the starch of green *mung* beans. May be soaked in hot water before use, or may require boiling according to the texture required. It is also deep fried straight from the packet, generally when used as a garnish or to provide a background for other foods.

CHILLI POWDER

Asian chilli powder is made from ground chillies. It is much hotter than the Mexican style chilli powder, which is mostly ground cummin.

CHILLI SAUCE

There are two different types of chilli sauce. The Chinese style is made from chillies, salt and vinegar, and has a hot flavour. The Malaysian, Singaporean or Sri Lankan chilli sauce is a mixture of hot, sweet and salty flavours generously laced with ginger and garlic and cooked with vinegar. It is easy to buy both types.

CHILLIES, BIRD'S EYE or BIRD PEPPERS

Very small, very hot chillies. Used mainly in pickles, though in some cases added to food when a very hot flavour is required (as in Thai food). Treat with extreme caution.

CHILLIES, CAPSICUM or PEPPERS
Bot.: *Capsicum frutescens or capsicum annum*
Fam.: *Solanaceae*
Sinhalese: *malu miris*

A much milder though still flavourful variety of chilli with a long pod large enough to stuff with spiced meat or fish mixtures.

CHILLIES, GREEN
Bot.: *Capsicum spp.*
Hindi: *subz mirich*
Sinhalese: *amu miris*
Thai: *nil thee sein*
Malay: *chilli, cabai hijau*
Indonesian: *lombok hijau*

Used like fresh red chillies. Sometimes ground into sambals. The seeds, which are the hottest parts, are usually (though not always) removed.

CHILLIES, RED
Bot.: *Capsicum* spp.
Hindi:*lal mirich*
Sinhalese: *rathu miris*
Burmese: *nil-thee*
Thai: *prik chee pha*
Tamil: *kochikai*
Malay: *cabai, chilli*
Indonesian: *lambok*

Used fresh for flavouring, either whole or finely chopped; or sliced for garnishes.

CINNAMON
Bot.: *Cinnamomum zeylanicum*
Fam.: *Lauraceae*
Hindi: *darchini*
Sinhalese: *kurundu*
Thai: *op chery*
Burmese: *thit-ja-boh-gauk*
Malay: *kayu manis*
Indonesian: *kayu manis*

True cinnamon is native to Sri Lanka. Buy cinnamon sticks or quills rather than the ground spice, which loses its flavour when stored too long. It is used in both sweet and savoury dishes.

Cassia, which is grown in India, Indonesia and Burma, is similar. It is much stronger in flavour, and is cheaper, but it lacks the delicacy of cinnamon. The leaves and buds of the cassia tree have a flavour similar to the bark and are also used for flavouring food.

For sweet dishes especially it is best to use true cinnamon. Look for the thin pale bark, sun-dried to form quills that are packed one inside the other. Cassia bark is much thicker because the corky layer is left on.

CLOVES
Bot.: *Eugenia aromatica*
Fam.: *Myrtaceae*
Hindi: *laung*
Sinhalese: *karabu*
Burmese: *ley-nyin-bwint*
Malay: *bunga cingkeh*
Indonesian: *cenkeh*

Cloves are the dried flower buds of an evergreen tropical tree native to Southeast Asia. They were used in China more than 2,000 years ago, and were also used by the Romans. Oil of cloves contains phenol, a powerful antiseptic that discourages putrefaction, and the clove is hence one of the spices that helps preserve food.

COCONUT MILK

Not the water inside the nut, as is commonly believed, but the creamy liquid extracted from the grated flesh of fresh coconuts or from desiccated (shredded) coconut. When coconut milk is called for, do try to use it, for the flavour cannot be duplicated by using any other kind of milk ,see page 9.

CORIANDER
Bot.: *Coriandrum sativum*
Fam.: *Umbelliferae*
Hindi: *dhania* (seed), *dhania pattar*,
   dhania sabz (leaves)
Sinhalese: *kottamalli* (seed),
   kottamalli kolle (leaves)
Burmese: *nannamzee* (seed),
   nannambin (leaves)
Thai: *pak chee*
Malay: *ketumbar* (seeds), *daun*
   ketumbar (leaves)

All parts of the coriander plant are used in Asian cooking. The dried seed is the main ingredient in curry powder, and although not hot it has a fragrance that makes it an essential part of a curry blend.

The fresh coriander herb is also called Chinese parsley or cilantro. Although it may take some getting used to because of its pungent smell (the name comes from the Greek *koris*, meaning 'bug'), Southeast Asian food is not the same without it. It is indispensable in Burma, Thailand, Vietnam, India and China where it is also called 'fragrant green'. If you have difficulty obtaining it, grow fresh coriander yourself in a small patch of garden or even a window box. Scatter the seeds, sprinkle lightly with soil and water every day. They take about 18 days to germinate. Pick them when about 15 cm (6 inches) high and do not allow plants to go to seed.

CUMMIN or CUMIN
Bot.: *Cuminum cyminum*
Fam.: *Umbelliferae*
Hindi: *sufaid zeera* (white cummin),
   zeera, jeera
Sinhalese: *sududuru*
Thai: *yira*
Malay: *jintan puteh*
Indonesian: *jinten*

Cummin is, with coriander, the most essential ingredient in prepared curry powders. It is available as seed, or ground. There is some confusion between cummin and caraway seeds because they are similar in appearance, but the flavours are completely different and one cannot replace the other in recipes.

CUMMIN, BLACK
Bot.: *Nigella sativa*
Fam.: *Ranunculaceae*
Hindi: *kala zeera, kalonji*

Although the Indian name *kala zeera* translates as 'black cummin' this is not true cummin and the flavour is different. Aromatic and peppery, *Nigella* is an essential ingredient in *panch phora*.

CUMMIN, SWEET

see fennel

CURRY LEAVES
Bot.: *Murraya koenigii*
Fam.: *Rutaceae*
Hindi: *kitha neem, katnim, karipattar*
Sinhalese: *karapincha*
Tamil: *karuvepila*
Burmese: *pyi-naw-thein*
Malay: *daun kari, karupillay*

Sold dried, they are as important to curries as bay leaves are to stews, but never try to substitute one for the other. The tree is native to Asia, the leaves are small and very shiny, and though they keep their flavour well when dried they are found in such abundance in Asia that they are generally used fresh. The leaves are fried in oil, until crisp, at the start of preparing a curry; they can also be pulverised in a blender; and the powdered leaves can be used in marinades and omelettes. Substitute *daun salam*.

CURRY POWDER

Rarely used in countries where curry is eaten daily (the word comes from the Tamil *Kari*, meaning 'sauce). It is preferable to roast and grind the spices separately.

DAUN PANDAN

see pandanus

DAUN SALAM

An aromatic leaf used in Indonesian cooking, it is larger than the curry leaf used in India and Sri Lanka, but has a similar flavour. Substitute curry leaves.

DILL
Bot.: *Anethum graveolens*
Fam.: *Umbelliferae*
Sinhalese: *enduru*

Much used in Russia and European cooking, this herb is also very popular in Sri Lanka where it gives a distinctive flavour to minced-meat mixtures, *frikkadels*, fish cutlets, and so on. Similar in appearance to fennel, it is much smaller and grows only to 45-90 cm (1½-3 feet) in height; the leaf is feathery and thread-like.

DRIED FISH
Hindi: *nethali*
Sinhalese: *haal masso*
Thai: *plasroi*
Malay: *ikan bilis*
Indonesian: *ikan bilis*

These tiny sprats or anchovies should be rinsed and the intestines removed (if this has not already been done) before use. Avoid soaking them, or they will not retain their crispness when fried. Dry on paper towels before frying.

DRIED SHRIMP PASTE
Burmese: *ngapi*
Thai: *kapi*
Malay: *blacan*
Indonesian: *trasi*

A pungent paste made from prawns, and used in many Southeast Asian recipes. It is sold in cans or flat slabs or cakes and will keep indefinitely. If stored in a tightly closed jar it will, like a genie in a bottle, perform its magic when required without obtruding on the kitchen at other times! It does not need refrigeration. Commercially sold as 'blachan' or 'belacan'.

FENNEL
Bot.: *Foeniculum vulgare*
Fam.: *Rutaceae*
Hindi: *sonf*
Sinhalese: *maduru*
Burmese: *samouk-saba*
Malay: *jintan manis*
Indonesian: *adas*

Sometimes known as 'sweet cummin' or 'large cummin', it is a member of the same botanical family and is used in Sri Lankan curries (but in much smaller quantities than true cummin). It is available in ground or seed form. Substitute an equal amount of aniseed.

FENUGREEK
Bot.: *Trigonella foenum-graecum*
Fam.: *Leguminosae* (papilionaceae)
Hindi: *methi*
Sinhalese: *uluhaal*
Malay: *alba*

These small, flat, squarish, brownish-beige seeds are essential in curries, but because they have a slightly bitter flavour they must be used in the stated quantities. They are especially good in fish curries, where the whole seeds are gently fried at the start of cooking; they are also ground and added to curry powders. The green leaves are used in Indian cooking and, when spiced, the bitter taste is quite piquant and acceptable. The plant is easy to grow, and when at the two-leaf stage it makes a tangy addition to salads.

FISH SAUCE
Burmese: *ngan-pya-ye*
Thai: *nam pla*

A thin, salty, brown sauce used in Southeast Asian cooking to bring out the flavour in other foods. A small variety of fish is packed in wooden barrels with salt, and the liquid that runs off is the 'fish sauce'. Substitute light soy sauce, adding to each cup one teaspoon of dried shrimp paste, which has been wrapped in foil and grilled for 5 minutes on each side and then powdered. Stir well and bottle. Shake bottle before use. There are different grades of fish sauce, the Vietnamese version being darker and having a more pronounced fish flavour than the others.

GALANGAL, GREATER
Bot.: *Alpinia galanga*
Fam.: *Zingiberaceae*
Thai: *kha*
Malay: *lengkuas*
Indonesian: *laos*

The greater galangal is more extensively used in Southeast Asian cooking than the lesser, and is more delicate in flavour. It is a rhizome, like ginger, and beneath the thin brown skin the flesh is creamy white; the flesh of lesser galangal has an orange-red hue.

GALANGAL, LESSER
Bot.: *Kaempferia pandurata* or
Alpinia officinarum
Fam.: *Zingiberaceae*
Sinhalese: *ingurupiyali*
Thai: *krachai*
Malay: *zeodary* or *kencur*
Indonesian: *kencur*

Also known as 'aromatic ginger', this member of the ginger family cannot be used as a substitute for ginger or vice versa. It is used only in certain dishes, and gives a pronounced aromatic flavour. When available fresh, it is sliced or pounded to a pulp; but outside of Asia it is usually sold dried, and the hard round slices must be pounded with a mortar and pestle or pulverised in a blender before use. In some spice ranges it is sold in powdered form. The plant is native to southern China and has been used for centuries in medicinal herbal mixtures, but it is not used in Chinese cooking.

GARAM MASALA

A mixture of ground spices used in Indian cooking.

GARLIC
Bot.: *Allium sativum*
Fam.: *Liliaceae*
Hindi: *lasan*
Sinhalese: *sudulunu*
Burmese: *chyet-thon-phew*
Malay: *bawang puteh*
Indonesian: *bawang putih*

Almost universal in application, and vital in Asian cooking (although Kasmiri Brahmins eschew it as inflaming baser passions), garlic is not only a flavouring but is also prized for its health-giving properties. There are many varieties — some with large cloves, some very small; some white in colour, some purplish; some easily peeled, and some with a skin that sticks so closely that it has to be prised off; and some are very strong in flavour, while other types can be quite mild.

GHEE (CLARIFIED BUTTER)

Sold in tins, *ghee*, is pure butter-fat without any of the milk solids. It can be heated to much higher temperatures than butter without burning, and imparts a distinctive flavour when used as a cooking medium.

GINGER
Bot.: *Zingiber officinale*
Hindi: *adrak*
Sinhalese: *inguru*
Burmese: *gin*
Thai: *khing*
Malay: *halia*
Indonesian: *jahe*

A rhizome with a pungent flavour, it is essential in most Asian dishes. Fresh ginger root should be used; powdered ginger cannot be substituted for fresh ginger, for the flavour is quite different. To prepare for use, scrape off the skin with a sharp knife, and either grate or crop finely (according to recipe requirements) before measuring. To preserve fresh ginger for long periods of time, scrape the skin from the rhizome, divide into sections and pack in a well-washed and dried bottle. Pour dry sherry over to completely cover the ginger, cover tightly and store in the refrigerator.

GROUND RICE

see rice, ground

KEMIRI NUTS

see candle nut

KEWRA

see *Pandanus odoratissimus*

LAOS
Bot.: *Alpinia galanga*

A very delicate spice, sold in powder form, *laos* comes from the dried root of the 'greater galangal'. It is so delicate in flavour that it can be omitted from recipes. See galangal.

LEMON GRASS
Bot.: *Cymbopogon citratus*
Fam.: *Gramineae*
Hindi: *sera*
Sinhalese: *sera*
Burmese: *zabalin*
Thai: *takrai*
Malay: *serai*
Indonesian: *sereh*

This aromatic Asian plant also grows in Australia, Africa, South America and Florida (USA). It is a tall grass with sharp-edged leaves that multiply into clumps. The whitish, slightly bulbous base is used to impart a lemony flavour to curries. Cut just one stem with a sharp knife, close to the root, and use about 10-12 cm (4-5 inches) of the stalk from the base, discarding the leaves. If using dried lemon grass, about 12 strips dried are equal to one fresh stem; or substitute 2 strips of very thinly peeled lemon rind.

LIME, SMALL GREEN
BOT.: *Citrus microcapa*
Hindi: *nimboo*
Sinhalese: *dehi*
Thai: *ma now*
Malay: *limau nipis, limau kesturi*

The juice of this fruit is used in Asian countries for adding a sour flavour to curries and other dishes. lemons may be used as a substitute.

MACE
Bot.: *Myristica fragrans*
Fam.: *Myristicaceae*
Hindi: *javatri*
Sinhalese: *wasa-vasi*

Mace is part of the nutmeg, a fruit that looks like an apricot and grows on tall tropical trees. When ripe, the fruit splits to reveal the aril, lacy and bright scarlet, surrounding the shell of the seed; the dried aril is mace and the kernel is nutmeg. Mace has a flavour similar to nutmeg but more delicate, and it is sometimes used in meat or fish curries, especially in Sri Lanka, although its main use in Asia is medicinal (a few blades of mace steeped in hot water, the water then being taken to combat nausea).

MALDIVE FISH
Sinhalese: *umbalakada*

Dried tuna from the Maldive Islands, used extensively in Sri Lankan cooking. It is sold in packets, broken into small chips, but needs to be pulverised further before use. Substitute dried prawn powder or Japanese *katsuobushi*.

MINT
Bot.: *Mentha viridis*
Fam.: *Labiatae*
Hindi: *podina*
Sinhalese: *meenchi*
Lao: *pak hom ho*
Malay: *daun pudina*

Although there are many varieties, the common, round-leafed mint is the one most often used in cooking. It adds flavour to many curries, and mint sambal is an essential accompaniment to a *biriani* meal or as a dipping sauce for *samoosa*. Mint is also used in Laotian fish dishes.

MUSHROOMS, STRAW
Bot.: *Volvariella volvacea*
Burmese: *hmo*

Also known as 'paddy straw mushrooms'. This tiny, cultivated mushroom consists of a sheath within which is the mushroom. Available canned, bottled or dried.

MUSTARD, BLACK
Bot.: *Brassica igra*
Fam.: *Crucilerae*
Hindi: *rai, kimcea* (brown mustard)
Sinhalese: *abba*
Malay: biji sawi

This variety of mustard seed is smaller and more pungent than the yellow variety. Substitute brown mustard seed (*juncia*). Alba or white mustard is not used in Asian cooking.

NUTMEG
Bot.: *Myristica fragrans*
Fam.: *Myristicaceae*
Hindi: *jaiphal*
Sinhalese: *sadikka*
Malay: *buah pala*
Indonesian: *pala*

Not widely used as a curry spice, but used to flavour some sweets and cakes, and sometimes used in *garam masala*. For maximum flavour, always grate finely just before using. Use sparingly, for larger quantities (more than one whole nut) can be poisonous.

ONION
Bot.: *Allium cepa*
Fam.: *Liliaceae*
Hindi: *peeaz*
Sinhalese: *lunu*
Malay: *bawang*
Thai: *hom hua lek*

Onions come in many varieties, but those most commonly used in Australia are the brown or white onions.

ONION, RED
Bot.: *Allium rubrum*

The most commonly used onions in Asia.

PALM SUGAR
Hindi: *jaggery*
Sinhalese: *hakuru*
Burmese: *tanyet* (Palmyrah),
  chandagar (cane)
Malay: *gula Melaka (Malacca)*
Indonesian: *gula Jawa*

This strong-flavoured dark sugar is obtained from the sap of coconut palms and Palmyrah palms. The sap is boiled down until it crystallises, and the sugar is usually sold in round, flat cakes or two hemispheres put together to form a ball and wrapped in dried leaves. Substitute black sugar, an unrefined, sticky sugar sold in health food stores, or use refined dark brown sugar sold at supermarkets.

PANCH PHORA

Panch means 'five' in Hindi, and *panch phora* is a combination of five different aromatic seeds. These are used whole, and when added to the cooking oil impart a flavour typical of Indian food.

PANDANUS or SCREWPINE
Bot.: *Pandanus latifolia*
Fam.: *Pandanaceae*
Sinhalese: *rampe*
Thai: *bai toey*
Malay: *daun pandan*
Indonesian: *daun pandan*

Used as a flavouring in rice, curries; and as à flavouring and colouring agent in Malay and Indonesian sweets. The long, flat, green leaves are either crushed or boiled to yield the flavour and colour. In Malaysia and Indonesia especially the flavour is as popular as vanilla is in the West.

PANDANUS ODORATISSIMUS
Hindi: *kewra*

Another variety of screwpine. The male inflorescence has a stronger perfume than roses or jasmin. It is used mostly in Indian sweets, and is obtainable as an essence or concentrate. It is so strong that only a drop is needed (or, more discreetly, a small skewer dipped in the essence is swished in the liquid to be flavoured). On special festive occasions, rose essence and kewra essence are used to flavour the rich rice dish, *biriani*.

PEPPER, BLACK
Bot.: *Piper nigrum*
Fam.: *Piperaceae*
Hindi: *kali mirich*
Sinhalese: *gammiris*
Burmese: *nga-yourk-kaun*
Malay: *lada hitam*
Indonesian: *merica hitam*

Pepper, the berry of a tropical vine, is green when immature, and red or yellow when ripe. Black pepper is obtained by sun-drying the whole berry. It is only used in some curries, but is an important ingredient in *garam masala*.

PEPPER, RED and GREEN
Bot.: *Capsicum grossum*
Sinhalese: *thakkali miris*

Also known as 'capsicums' and 'sweet' or 'bell' peppers, this large, rounded variety is very mild and sweet in flavour, and is used as a vegetable or salad ingredient.

POPPY SEEDS
Bot.: *Papaver somniferum*
Fam.: *Papaveraceae*
Hindi: *khas-khas*

Used in Indian curries mainly for thickening gravies since flour, cornflour or other starches are never used for thickening. The seeds are ground to a powder for this use.

PRAWN POWDER

Finely shredded dried prawns or shrimps, sold in packets at specialty food shops and at Chinese grocery stores.

RAMPE

see pandanus

RICE, GROUND

This can be bought at many grocery stores, health food stores and supermarkets, and is slightly more granular than rice flour. It gives a crisper texture when used in batters or other mixtures.

RICE VERMICELLI
Chinese: *mei fun*
Malay: *beehoon, meehoon*
Thai: *sen mee*

Sometimes labelled 'rice sticks', these are very fine rice flour noodles sold in Chinese grocery stores. Soaking in hot water for 10 minutes prepares them sufficiently for most recipes, but in some cases they may need boiling for one or two minutes. When deep fried they swell up and turn white. For a crisp result, fry them straight from the packet without soaking.

ROSE WATER

A favourite flavouring in Indian and Persian sweets, rose water is the diluted essence extracted from rose petals by steam distillation. If you use rose essence or concentrate, be careful not to over-flavour — count the drops. However, with rose water a tablespoon measure can be used. Buy rose water from chemists or from shops specialising in Asian ingredients.

ROTI FLOUR

Creamy in colour and slightly granular in texture, this is ideal flour for all unleavened breads; unlike *atta* flour, it is not made from the whole grain. Sold at some health food and Chinese grocery stores.

SAFFRON
Bot.: *Crocus sativus*
Fam.' *Iridaceae*
Hindi: *kesar*

The world's most expensive spice, saffron is obtained by drying the stamens of the saffron crocus. The thread-like strands are dark orange in colour and have a strong perfume; it is also available in powder form. Do not confuse it with turmeric, which is sometimes sold as 'Indian saffron'. Beware also of cheap saffron, which in all probability will be safflower or 'bastard saffron' — it looks similar, and imparts colour, but has none of the authentic fragrance. Saffron is used more extensively in northern India than anywhere else in Asia.

SAMBAL ULEK

A combination of chillies and salt, used in cooking or as an accompaniment. The old Dutch-Indonesian spelling, still seen on some labels, is 'sambal oelek'.

SESAME SEED
Bot.: *Sesamum indicum*
Fam.: *Pedaliaceae*
Hindi: *till*
Sinhalese: *thala*
Malay: *bijan*

Used mostly in Korean, Chinese and Japanese food, and in sweets in Southeast Asian countries. Black sesame, another variety known as *hak chih mah* (China) or *kuro goma* (Japan), is mainly used in the Chinese dessert, toffee apples, and as a flavouring (*gomasio*) mixed with salt in Japanese food.

SESAME OIL

The sesame oil used in Chinese cooking is extracted from toasted sesame seeds, and gives a totally different flavour from the lighter-coloured sesame oil sold in health food stores. For the recipes in this book, buy sesame oil from Chinese stores. Use the oil in small quantities for flavouring, not as a cooking medium.

SHALLOTS
Bot.: *Allium ascalonicum*

Shallots are small, purplish onions with red-brown skin. Like garlic, they grow in a cluster and resemble garlic cloves in shape. The name 'shallots' in Australia is generally (and incorrectly) given to spring onions.

SHRIMP PASTE, DRIED

see dried shrimp paste

SPRING ONIONS (SCALLIONS or GREEN ONIONS)
Bot.: *Allium cepa* or *Allium fistulum*
Fam.: *Liliaceae*

This member of the onion family is known as 'shallot' in Australia, but is correctly called a spring onion almost everywhere else (though the term 'scallion' is popular in the USA). Spring onions are the thinnings of either *Allium cepa* or *A. fistulum* plantings that do not form a bulb. They are white and slender, with green leaves, and are used widely in China and Japan.

TAMARIND
Bot.: *Tamarindus indica*
Fam.: *Leguminoseae*
Hindi: *imli*
Sinhalese: *siyambala*
Malay: *asam*
Indonesian: *asam*
Thai: *som ma kham*

This acid-tasting fruit of a large tropical tree is shaped like a large broad bean and has a brittle brown shell, inside which are shiny dark seeds covered with brown flesh. Tamarind is dried, and sold in packets. For use as acid in a recipe, soak a piece the size of a walnut in half a cup of hot water for 5-10 minutes until soft, then squeeze it until it mixes with the water and strain out the seeds and fibres. Tamarind liquid is used in given quantities.

TURMERIC .
Bot.: *Curcuma Longa*
Fam.: *Zingiberaceae*
Hindi: *haldi*
Sinhalese: *kaha*
Burmese: *fa nwin*
Indonesian: *kunyit*
Thai: *kamin*

A rhizome of the ginger family, turmeric with its orange-yellow colour is a main stay or commercial curry powders. Though often called Indian saffron, it should never be confused with true saffron and the two may not be used interchangeably.

WOOD FUNGUS
Bot.: *Auricalaria polytricha*
Chinese: *wun yee*
Japanese: *kikurage*
Malay: *kuping tikus*
Indonesian: *kuping jamu*
Thai: *hed henu*

Also known as 'cloud ear fungus' or 'jelly mushrooms', wood fungus is sold by weight, and in its dry state looks like greyish-black pieces of paper. Soaked in hot water for 10 minutes, it swells to translucent brown shapes like curved clouds or a rather prettily shaped ear — hence the name 'cloud ear fungus'. With its flavourless resilience it is a perfect example of a texture ingredient, adding no taste of its own but taking no subtle flavours from the foods with which it is combined. Cook only for a minute or two.

YOGHURT

Cultured yoghurt. For recipes in this book, use unflavoured yoghurt (preferably one with a pronounced acid flavour) such as Greek yoghurt or goat's milk yoghurt.

INDEX

Flaky Wholemeal Bread (Paratha) 30
Fragrant Spice Powder 21
Fresh Coriander of Coconut
    Chutney 108
Fresh Lemon Grass Salad 106
Fresh Mint Chutney 102
Fresh Peanut Curry 94
Fried Chilli Sambal 103
Fried Eggplant Sambol 111
Fried Pork Curry 46
Fried Squid Curry 63

G
Garam Masala 21
Ghee Rice 26
Glutinous Yellow Rice 27
Green Curry of Duck 85
Green Curry of Fish 58
Green Curry Paste 15
Green Masala Paste 16
Ground Onion & Chilli Sambol 105

H
Handling of Chillies 9
Hot Beef Curry 43
Hot Chicken Curry 81
Hot Fish Curry with Shrimp Paste 62
Hot Pork Curry 47
Hundred Almond Curry 78

J
Javanese Chicken Curry 79
Javanese Minced Steak Curry 40

K
Kofta Curry 39

L
Lamb Korma 45
Lentil Purée 99
Liver Curry (Malaysia) 50
Liver Curry (Sri Lanka) 50
Long Beans of Tomato Curry 94

M
Madras Chicken Curry 75
Madras Curry Paste 15
Madras Curry Powder 16

Madras Mutton Curry 45
Madras Prawn Curry 64
Malay Vegetable Pickles 112
Meat & Potato Curry 36
Minced Meat & Potato Curry 41
Moghul Vegetable Curry 98
Moslem Beef Curry 40
Mushroom & Potato Curry 96
Moslem Chicken Curry 82
Moslem Curry Paste 18

N
Nepalese Pea & Potato Curry 93
Noodles:
    Rice, with curry 26

O
Oil Rice 28
Omelette Curry 86
Omelette Sambal 106
Onion & Tomato Sambal 104

P
Padang Duck Curry 85
Panch Phora 21
Pappadams 111
Piquant Fried Prawn Sambal 106
Pork Curry 49
Pork Curry, Dry 48
Pork Padre Curry 48
Pork Vindaloo 47
Potato Curry 95
Poultry Curry Paste 17
Pounded Prawn Paste 105
Prawn & Sweet Gourd Curry 65
Prawn Blachan 107
Prawn Coconut Milk Curry 66
Prawn Curry, Dry 66
Prawn Curry (India) 67
Prawn Curry (Malaysia) 68
Prawn Curry with Gravy 64
Prawn Red Curry 68
Prawn Vindaloo 68
Pumpkin & Coconut Curry 99

R
Rabbit Curry 87
Red Coconut Sambol 104

Red Curry of Beef 35
Red Curry Paste 18
Red Prawn Curry 67
Rice:
    Coconut 26, Cooked in Coconut Milk
    with Spices 29, Cooked in Stock with
    Spices 28, Ghee 26, Glutinous
    Yellow 27, Oil 28, Savoury with
    Lentils 25, Steamed 24, Thai Fried
    27, White 24, Yellow 25
Rice cooked in Coconut Milk with
    Spices 29
Rice cooked in Stock with Spices 28
Rice Noodles with Curry 26
Roasted Coconut Sambol 111

S
Salt Fish & Eggplant Curry 65
Sambal Udang 106
Satay Curry 41
Savoury Rice with Lentils 25
Shrimp Paste Saute 107
Skewered Mutton Curry 44
Spiced Spinach 103
Spicy Cabbage in Coconut Milk 95
Spicy Mutton Curry 44
Spinach and Cheese Curry 98
Squid Curry 58
Steamed Rice 24
Sumatran Beef Curry 42

T
Thai Fried Rice 27
Tomato & Spring Onion Sambal 108
Tripe Curry 51

V
Vegetable Curry (Malaysia) 97
Vegetable Curry (Sri Lanka) 96

W
White Rice 24

Y
Yellow Pumpkin Curry 93
Yellow Rice 25

Seafood makes delicious curries. The recipe for this Crab Curry is on page 69.